Collecting True Friends

Be a Magnet to Those Worthy of Your Time and Devotion

by Elizabeth Duncan-Hawker

☆ May your world be Blessed with True friends!

+ God Bless

Elizabeth

Published by Woodhouse Publishing

ISBN: 978-0-578-99265-5

FOREWORD

When asked to write the foreword to Elizabeth Duncan-Hawker's inaugural *Collecting True Friends,* I was surprised. Why me? Wouldn't someone with relevant credentials be a better choice? How about one of her lifelong friends—to showcase the mad strength and effectiveness of Ms. Duncan-Hawkers' friendship making skills?

It took me a minute, but then I realized Elizabeth's genius. Who better to present this compendium of personal anecdotes on the importance of friendship and actionable steps to create a life rich with relationships than someone who has directly experienced and been recently and quickly "won over" by Ms. Duncan-Hawker herself?

I met Elizabeth eight months ago on the chat-only social media app Clubhouse. As the CEO and founder of Kuel Life, a platform created for women 45-plus dedicated to normalizing aging through highly curated content and women-driven brands, I began using Clubhouse as a way to elevate the conversation among our Second Act Sisters. Elizabeth showed up immediately in the club room, ready to share, learn and play with us all. From our initial conversation, I knew there was something special about her. Immediately, I picked up on the skill with which she asked questions, shared her experiences, and furthered the conversation. The sparks flew.

Before I knew it, I found myself virtually meeting Elizabeth alone and using those sparks to make magic. In a short eight months, I can call *Red Hawk* (a community nickname so befitting her) a friend. Yes, it's a newish, still-blossoming relationship. But based on the building blocks evident from its inception, I can tell you it is the real deal. Elizabeth walks her walk, and she does it in an unapologetically bold way. She practices what she preaches, and the evidence is seen in her impressive portfolio of high-caliber friendships.

The value of good friendships is not new news. More than 100 years' worth of research has shown that people with supportive, healthy, connected relationships live longer than those without. In one seven-year study, the research participants with larger social networks—regardless of their socioeconomic status, smoking, drinking or exercise habits, or body mass index—were about 45 percent less likely to die than those with smaller friend groups.

Turns out loneliness is as lethal as smoking fifteen cigarettes a day. Ouch.

How does Duncan-Hawker do it? In a room full of cowboys, Elizabeth dons the brightest, most colorful boots and a ten-gallon hat. As a military brat, Elizabeth moved incessantly. Seven times before high school. She figured out early in life to have a solid, extensive tribe of true friends you would need to take action. And action she took. And unintentionally developing highly sought-after skills in the process. Luckily for us, Elizabeth felt called to share her knowledge and expertise.

In these pages, Duncan-Hawker crafts more than a tale on the importance of friendships. She regales us with beautiful personal narratives, then engages us with questions and opportunities to reflect what Duncan-Hawker has termed Pondering Pauses, allowing the reader to internalize and personalize the experience of this book.

Elizabeth gives us the perfect "guidebook" to develop our own personal strategy for collecting our tribe of true friends. Each chapter takes us through the importance of a particular skill and offers us ways to implement them. Through the book she offers Pondering Pauses and specific exercises, encouraging the reader to take pencil to paper. With pragmatic strategies and practice strategies for how and where to look for friendships, how to evaluate if a friendship is the real deal, ways to take the lead in creating your inner circle, all the way through identifying and surviving relationships with an expiration date, you'll find that Duncan-Hawker provides just the right amount of handholding so we can strategically create our own personal board of directors.

Many of us grew up thinking that finding, making and maintaining friendships was a passive exercise—something that just *happens* to us. Elizabeth is here to tell us there is nothing automatic about this process. It takes active engagement and commitment. There's no way around the work. But when we remember the life-saving properties that true connection affords us, having a personal guidebook on updating our mindset and methods of connecting with others is truly the best health insurance policy.

Yours Truly,

Jacqueline (Jack) Perez
CEO/Founder of Kuel Life
www.kuellife.com

TABLE OF CONTENTS

DEDICATION

I dedicate this book to my mother "Betsy" who demonstrates we can all make friends everywhere, my loving husband "Donald" who always believes in everything I do, my smart, loving, fun, daughters, grandkids, nieces and family, and to each of my treasured friends "collected" along my life journey. To God be the Glory.

Elizabeth

PREFACE
GOODBYE TO THE GIRL WITH THE BIGGEST SMILE

"How could she have kept her cancer a secret?"

My head was numb, and our conversation repeated over and over. I could not process what I was hearing, and yet it was terrifying and oh so real. I was frowning with confusion as her words replayed in my head like a bad song you can't stop humming.

"Olsen, why didn't you tell me?" I asked.

"Because your dad had just died, and you couldn't handle it, that's why," she slowly shared.

"Ugh!" I yelled. Then my head filled with so many questions. "When are you seeing an oncologist? Should we postpone our girl's trip this week to Miami? When's your next doctor appointment?"

Olsen said, "We can still go on our trip. My oncologist appointment is six weeks away."

I sat stunned in disbelief. Not only am I hearing my dear friend, godmother to my children, has aggressive cancer, but her earliest appointment is in six weeks to see her specialist. "Are you kidding me? That is forever to wait! Just how big is this lump?" I asked, needing answers.

That was one of those unforgettable days. Time simply stood still. Shock powered down my brain to slowly process the severity of the news. Shock does that to get us through the danger at hand. Little did we realize the level of danger ahead.

Then Life Happens

Funny how you can be hyper-focused on one thing, and then something else unknown kicks you in the butt. Death rarely comes at a convenient time. Two months before our girls' trip, my dad suddenly died in his sleep at 72 years old, leaving us with a mess of affairs. It was surreal how someone can be there one minute and gone the next. Daddy and I had talked on the phone at midnight about his birthday party and luncheon the next day. I had my car filled with gifts and balloons, and as soon as the kids woke up, we were heading over. Yet, within hours of us talking, he passed. My world imploded, and nothing made sense. Olsen always had my back. So naturally, she just stepped up and was our family rock, preparing us for the funeral in only two days. She ran herself ragged, taking my girls to get dresses, a new suit for my husband, consoling us, and arranging a reception.

Olsen keenly saw how stunned I was from Daddy's death. That's why she kept her secret. How afraid she must have been that within just ten days, the big "C" had doubled her one breast in size, making it as hard as a softball underneath. Yet, her determination and bravery were undeniable.

Miami, Here We Come

We planned our getaway so long ago and started counting down the days. Both of us worked crazy long hours and cared for our busy families, so getting away from daily responsibilities always recharged us. We would email each other a daily countdown in the subject line for a fun twist of excitement. We were going to cram so much fun into our five days away.

Our girl's vacation trip was finally happening, yet there was a dark cloud hovering over us. Olsen grew up in Miami, where the sun, oranges, and the beach were a way of life. She couldn't wait to take me there to meet her youngest sister and explore the Florida Keys. Her last visit home was to bury her older sister who had not beaten cancer. Cancer ran in her family, yet somehow, we believed it would never hit her, too. We may have thought it, but never mentioned it aloud.

Off We Go

At the airport, I gave Olsen a diamond cross necklace I had Father Cristiano bless. Somehow, I naively hoped that would ensure she would be alright. Olsen beamed, latching the shiny cross around her neck, smiled, and we ran to catch the plane.

Miami was great fun, just like we dreamed. Rum punches on the beach with her sister, dancing at the open-style bars along the strip and laughing at the bizarre nightlife. We even saw the Everglades on a crazy fast airboat, then darted off to see the famous Florida Keys.

Time seemed too fast forward to the Fall season, and my dear friend had a successful mastectomy. Her margins looked fine. We jumped, cheering when we heard such great news. We grabbed our hubbies and headed to the Caribbean to celebrate. We embraced lots of firsts on that trip. Whatever Olsen selected for excursions, we agreed. We rode horses in the water, drank rum punches in the ocean, shopped in the villages, laughed, and acted silly all day and night.

One night, the Bahama beach air was so muggy, and I could see she was hot. "It's time to ditch the wig," I said with a smile. I complimented how beautifully round her head was with her new short grey hair look. She missed her long red hair. Since we both were Scandinavian, with long limbs, big smiles, and red hair, most strangers assumed we were related. We'd playfully agree that we were sisters.

Feeling like the worst was behind Olsen, the Christmas holidays were extra happy. Peace and joy were ours. She played and cooked with her goddaughters. My relationship with Olsen was a rare gift, so special that I trusted her to help in the delivery room when my girls were born. She held them moments after their birth and loved them like the babies she could never have.

Then a fierce winter blew in, and one day she suddenly felt hot and slightly off. We often talked, so when she called my office, I was thrilled to hear her voice until she said, "Things aren't feeling right." The prognosis was wrong. There was cancer now in her liver.

"What?" I screamed and collapsed to my knees on my office floor, unable to breathe.

Harsh Reality

We brought a hot meal that she couldn't eat. We sat on her couch, not knowing what to say, except to declare we should book the Paris trip now instead of waiting for her 50th birthday. Then, finally, my dear, sweet, sister of a friend slowly raised her head, pursed her lips, winced, and quietly said, "There will be no more travel." At that moment, I knew what she knew; death was looming.

I got busy on the phone and insisted her mother, father, and sister come up from Florida at our expense. They needed to get here, now. They arrived within days, yet I could see in their eyes the denial. It was too hard to accept that another daughter was fighting for her life. They struggled to accept Olsen as she now was, fading and shutting down. Once more, time stood still.

The very day of my mother's housewarming was the day God decided He needed Olsen. Ironically, she had insisted on helping plan the entire house-warming that she would not attend. My mother had picked that date as a respectful year, marking my father's death. It was to be a celebration for my mom, who relocated into our neighborhood. But, instead, that day, as fate would have it, I held one of my dearest friends in my arms for the last time.

Say Good-bye to Her Big Smile

I left my mom's housewarming to return to Olsen's hospital bed. The many tubes caused her discomfort and despair, and yet her face softened when we walked in. I could tell she felt joy seeing we were back. Earlier in the day, before we left to set up my mom's house, I had hugged her and told her how much I loved her.

She clearly said, "I love you, TOO!" But now, she could no longer speak.

Day turned to night; Olsen waited for her husband to leave the room. As she intensely stared at me, I knew what was happening. When you share a bond with a friend this deeply, you learn to understand the meanings behind a nod or a smile. I knew it was her time. I sensed Olsen could see someone over in the corner of the room. I imagined it was her sister who died the year prior.

I leaned over and cradled her in my arms. Olsen looked up to the left and softly smiled with peace. I whispered a promise we'd watch over her husband Chuck and asked her to watch over our three girls. She nodded, I nodded. I bit my lip, and with tears dropping, gave in to the inevitable.

"Now, go to that Angel you see; it's alright. I've got you. I am here. May God bless you," I whispered in her ear. It's hard to explain how I could sense what she needed and wanted—which was my blessing to ascend. Her chest fell, and there was a long pause in time.

The girl with the world's biggest smile was gone.

I never dreamed she'd die in my arms; what an honor to have that level of trust that she could surrender and let me help her pass onto heaven. To this day, to celebrate Olsen's life, I wear around my neck the cross I gave her. I am living on, and I believe as long as you say the name of a departed loved one, they live on, too.

Losing the Ones We Love

Within fourteen months, my father died in his sleep, and my young friend (godmother to my children) died peacefully in my arms. But, as I've said, Olsen was not merely my dear friend; she was family. We shared our dreams, struggles, childbirths, and through it all, she loved me, faults and all. Those included our best and worst times over two decades. We were vulnerable and open with each other, sharing a determination to make each other better. Being vulnerable means surrendering your ego, knowing you trust someone to be there for you, regardless of what happens. A jewel of a friend like that is a rarity. She was a true friend.

My Intent for You, The Reader

When you experience something so devastating, it makes you question what is truly important. If you have a deep connection to a friend now, embrace that person and let them know how deeply you value your friendship and work harder to bring value to them. Wisdom should guide you to stop and see who you would dearly miss, what you can do for them, and what is missing in your life.

Everyone should feel that level of love in a friendship at least once in their life and, if blessed, multiple times.

As I looked back on my closeness with Olsen and my current dear friends, I realized there was a method to creating great friendships. The art of finding, developing, and keeping amazing friendships CAN be learned. If you've had it and lost it, realize what you had and shared, remembering it as a treasure. If you have some close friendships, remember to cherish them.

For thousands of years, humans across all cultures shared experience and wisdom through stories. As a result, I share many stories in this book to highlight the needed skills that gain and keep friendships. Learning how to be a fantastic friend and recognize a potential friend worthy of you requires a specific set of skills. Those connecting skills, human to human, will reward you throughout your life, if embraced.

Collecting friends is an ART that fills your world with laughter and substance and once enjoyed, can be addictive. It is addictive because your life becomes fulfilled, making you want to surround yourself with an abundance of more authentic friends.

Welcome to the Concept and Art of Collecting True Friends in Your World!

After finishing this preface, I invite you to read this book in your preferred style and at your own pace. You can approach this book by reading cover to cover for layered learning or read the chapters most urgently needed in your life right now.

Answer the PONDERING PAUSE questions fully, if possible, or think about it and come back. Take some time to really study and update any dormant skills in your current friendship making world to make them better. That's when you will know what to practice becoming a better friend and identify those who are worthy of your efforts.

Ideally, you should spend more time on the topics that touch your heart and mind. So jump into this book, be open to its messages, and absorb its pieces of truth. My wish for you, my dear reader, is to learn how to be a fantastic true friend and attract the same into your life. Remember, friendships are meant to yield great enjoyment in life. I want you to experience more of the treasured friendships that last a lifetime.

Think of *Collecting True Friends* as an action-oriented journey. Learn the lessons, apply them, and reap the benefits. Life is not a dress rehearsal. Make the most of it and have some fun along the way while *Collecting True Friends*.

A yellow rose is the sign of friendship.

CHAPTER 1
THE *LITTLE VIKING GIRL*

Like a phoenix rising from the ashes, sometimes the challenges we face in childhood yield unexpected bonuses. With a father in the military, we moved seven times before I was 13 years old. Uprooting one's life from city to city and experiencing many cultures and climates requires extreme perseverance and tenacity to make friends and fit in. When you don't look like anyone around you, bullying becomes a norm in your life, which could lead to loneliness and isolation. Those challenges in my childhood led me to develop superior relationship making skills. Thus, I learned the mindset and art of collecting true friends.

I was bullied not only for being the "new" kid, but also for how starkly different I looked with my flaming red hair, pale skin, big freckles, and gangly legs. The combo just made me stand out—a Viking in current times. I was so fair that I looked overexposed in every school classroom photo. When I met strangers, I might as well have told them I was from another world. Maybe that would have made more sense to the locals, bewildered by the odd-looking new kid. Instead of appearing intriguing to others, I seemed bizarre. That was a huge challenge to accept as a child.

The Price of Not Blending with Strangers
Few looked like me; I don't recall ever having a ginger friend until after college, ever! I represent 1% of the world population, a legit combo of recessive genes in the human DNA. No one knew I was a mutant anomaly of genetics in nature. They just thought I was bizarre looking. Not being like anyone else plus always being the "new kid" in a school or neighborhood kept my awareness on high alert. This awareness made me develop an ability to spot people with genuinely lovely character. It's like an intuitive superpower. I also created a sensitivity for spotting cruelty. You get a feeling in your bones who is genuine and not, which

is known as discernment. Decades passed before I even knew what that term meant. Well-developed discernment skills and awareness abilities are a blessing to identify people worthy of potential friendship.

Be Careful What You Wish For
As a kid, I hated my freckles so much and wished to have the lovely, bronzed skin I saw on the other girls. When summer came, the sun contrasted their hair and skin even more, which made them appear even prettier, or so it seemed. The other kids bronzed, while I got another shade of dark pink then burned. I thought, how exotic and beautiful everyone else appeared.

One day, I took a hard fall while playing hopscotch and slid nose first onto the concrete. For the next three months, I sported a road rash across my entire nose. Seriously! I didn't stand out enough, and that made me even more noticeable. You can imagine how I looked with a crusty scab for my nose! It was so gross that the school photographer posed me sideways to take my class photo. Hilarious right? I believe we can manifest something if we want it to happen, and I did in this case. I hated my freckles and BAM they were gone. When my nose fully recovered, it was beautifully blank of those giant spots. God's wink was all over that incident. Something ugly turned into something beautiful for me.

When you don't fit in with others, every day is another day to keep your guard up, waiting for something to go sideways. Perhaps you, too, have experienced this feeling. Luckily, I was pretty smart and made some friends because I focused on mastering different hobbies, like dressing up our dogs, searching for moose tracks, bullfrog hunting in ponds, board games, racing bikes, and bird watching. I found that doing cool things can make you even more of a magnet to others, and then they ignore your weird looks. This method is a great skill I still use and recommend. People are intrigued by others who have unusual hobbies.

Conform—Culture Shock

Moving seven times before High School made life feel like a constant reboot. As soon as I settled in with a routine, knew my bike routes, got settled in school, and made new friends, my dad got orders, and we were back on the road. It felt like we were gypsies. Constant relocations meant survival mode had to kick in quickly. The way I saw it, I had two choices. I could either become a loner and stay in a shell like a turtle, or risk sticking my head out. I learned how to make friends and did so time and time again. I proved to myself that friendships were possible, even though it took a lot of work. I learned it did not matter what anyone looked like or spoke like. If they were nice people and fun to be around, I'd like to be friends. It was simple. Parents can't be at school to fix everything or protect us from all of life's challenges. That philosophy rings true for all of us in life. Only we can change how we want things to be tomorrow and with whom we surround ourselves.

Don't Look Back

You can't live a happy life by looking backward. There were many times I would gaze off daydreaming during class and remember leaving California's warm sunny coastline and feeling sad we left. I was young and confused why we had to leave such a beautiful place. The San Diego air was soft; it hardly rained. I could walk to school each day, my fluffy white poodle and I played in the yard with my friends, and life was easy. So, when my sweet mom said we had to pack and go live in freezing Maine, it felt like they sent us to another planet. Like a banishment, the car ride seemed like a month. My brother Bo and I stretched out in the back of the station wagon. I still remember the long days and nights as we drove through fields and mountains. Bo was even more upset; he left behind a world of hot sand, cute girls, and surfing at Imperial Beach with his buddies. Life was simple and fun for him, too. In between surfing, they'd fish and cook on a beach bonfire. Talk about a culture shock! No wonder my mind would drift back to that happier, sunnier home.

Culture Shocks

The relocations continued, and I forged on meeting and making new friends, surrounded by the constant bullying. The climate changes were extremely harsh, and people were not so warm either. Back in California, my friends knew how to pronounce an "r" when they spoke, which made me laugh when in Maine and Boston they said I was the person talking funny. What a constant life of culture shocks! Each state we lived in introduced unique accents, rules, and traditions that seemed odd until I conformed. Up north, you never called anyone "Ma'am or Sir" since that was considered a sign of disrespect (ageism). It was equivalent to calling a woman an old maid if she was not married. Miss or mister was the appropriate salute. Fast forward to our next move to the south, which brought more culture shocks. Teachers and neighbors expected to hear "Ma'am" as a proper salutation; if you don't know that social rule, BAM! They thought you had poor manners. Geez!

Fitting In . . . Insulate Your World

Along the way, I learned how to identify and emulate what others considered "good manners." I realized early on that making a great first impression made it so much easier to fit in, cutting down on the bullying. When you don't stick out in a crowd, the jerks are less likely to target you for ridicule. Likewise, I learned the power of having friends. Friendships insulate you from more attacks. That radiant energy generated from friendships shields your psyche from idiots trying to bring you down. They say God doesn't give us anything we can't handle. Yet, back then I thought He over estimated my capabilities! That challenging journey led me to who I became and now to share this wisdom with you. Today, I thank God for showing me the necessity of collecting the right people as friends and mentors.

You Never See Yourself How Others See You

Surprisingly, something weird happened when I became a teenager. The student's perception of me changed. The bullying stopped. Plus, another great blessing occurred. I found a best friend for life. A tall beauty named Terri showed kindness to this "new kid" sitting behind her in French class. Our friendship bonded quickly, and today she is still my treasured friend. She became my insulation and helped me assimilate into my latest world of change.

Years later, during our high school 20th reunion, I was astonished to learn they had voted me "Most Confident during High School." They had never told me. I laughed so loudly when they casually mentioned it. I would have loved to have known about this award since I had no clue others saw me as being that strong. Seriously? No one had any idea how stressed I was living at home with an alcoholic father. I kept that news shocker to myself, believing it wasn't anyone's business. Others just needed to see the polished persona I presented. That same irony is used and practiced on Facebook every day. People present a version of themselves they craft to show the world. It doesn't mean someone is a fake. It does mean they are controlling what we see about them. They saw a young woman who created an outward appearance of a big smile proudly walking tall at school.

I learned early watching how others responded nicer to those who stood tall, shoulders back and heads up. As a result, they were less targeted to ridicule. It was my survival strategy. Once bullied, constantly aware! When I was very young, I desperately wanted to blend in, and as I aged, I finally saw that was not the best approach. It is much better to be true to yourself. Being a copycat holds you back from defining who you are meant to be. Being genuine is a trait that draws in great friendships because uniqueness attracts others more than ordinariness.

PONDERING PAUSE – REFLECT AND THEN FILL IN YOUR ANSWERS:

- When people see me, I think they see _____ and _____traits.
- The traits my new friends are most surprised to find out about me are _____ and _____ which are usually not known until they get to know me better.
- I think these traits serve me well in life. Yes____ No____
- I will choose these traits _____, _____, _____to embrace or express more now on.
- I will choose to abandon these traits _____, _____, _____ because they no longer serve my best interest.
- I thought my friends knew I possess the trait of _____yet they seemed surprised when they saw me _____. (Example: you have a great ability to negotiate or solve a puzzle)

A Gift Learned by Always Being the New Kid - the *Little Viking Girl*
To this day, I am sensitive to how hard it is for others (of all ages) to make a friend, join a group, meeting, or event. Not knowing anyone when you enter a room and trying to mix with strangers is one of the hardest things humans can encounter. So, in 2018, I felt compelled to start a training service to help professionals mix easier when meeting others (www.GrowthNetworking.com). As a kid and now, I find one of the best ways to make a new friend is to be that amazing person who shows compassion and guides newcomers in their new environment. It could be at work, a meeting, an event, a school, a neighborhood, a church, a club, a party, etc., that someone needs your grace. Identifying a person struggling is only the first step towards being stellar at collecting true friends. Deciding to take action and show them grace and assistance is what puts you above the rest. It also demonstrates confidence and resilience to others. Those are key to drawing others to lean in with interest when you speak.

Likewise, when watching out for others, we also need to remember we are continually observed. Many people observe our behaviors from afar to determine if they want to know us. Sadly, we may never even get the chance to meet these fantastic people because they make a choice based on what they first witnessed. I see people often unaware of how their actions (good and bad) determine if friendships will follow. Whether you are backing out of a driveway, letting someone cut into traffic, choosing a parking space, walking into a building, or standing in the elevator, all actions are observed. It repels others from us when we act in haste or rudely, much like a magnet repels and attracts.

I've seen from a distance others make up their minds if they want to talk to me or get to know me better. If they are unsure, I ask myself what I can do to bring value to that person. Then, I put my thinking cap on. It could be something easy, like they need a sitter's phone number or help with the charity they love. Being thoughtful is like a ray of golden sunshine around you. It draws others to inquire, "Who is that nice person?" They may approach you the next time and "lean in" to listen when you speak. An essential part of our self-awareness development is to realize others are always watching us. Never forget that. Make it a point this week to stop and help someone else and notice how others are watching your actions.

Takeaways to Consider When Meeting Others

Bullied kids grow into adults that you might want to become friends with, and that might not be easy at first. Some may still believe those stupid taunts and labels. It might have destroyed their self-confidence even though they now appear polished to the world. Grab onto this as truth. Just because someone seems attractive or successful now does not mean they don't want your approval, affirmation, or endorsement. In most cases, they would like to hear that you'd like to be their friend. Likewise, they may think you are too smart, pretty, rich, poor, young, old, or different looking to be friends. As adults, others may be intimidated and think we would not be interested in getting to know them. Why? Because they still see themselves as that little kid no one befriended. Crazy! Right? Yet so true.

Here is what you must remember to do. If you spot someone you'd like to know better, share what intrigues you. People bullied in their past can act guarded at first when becoming a new friend. Trust is the vital element that must be earned so you can move forward knowing them better. I cover more on this subject in Chapter 5 (Roadblocks to True Friendships). Understanding and observing local norms and customs makes it easier to attract friends quicker. Likewise, your life is easier when you assimilate into new places because others are more accepting. Particularly remember that if you don't look like you belong somewhere, fitting in quickly is your goal, just like me, the *Little Viking Girl.*

PONDERING PAUSE:

- I can recall when I was the stranger at the _____ place.
- Can I remember the person's name (or face) who befriended me? ___Yes ___No
- When they talked to me and helped me meet others, I felt _____ emotions. *(Describe how it felt in your heart and mind.)*
- Am I still connected with the kind person who welcomed me as a stranger? Did the person become my friend? ___Yes ___No
- Would I consider reconnecting to let them know I appreciated them? ___Yes ___No *Magic can happen when you share your gratitude.*
- When spotting a newcomer, I can make them feel more welcome if I _____.

Adopt The Mindset of *Collecting True Friends*

Growing up and never blending in with others, I finally learned it is always better to be YOU because we all are unique, even though we all try to fit in. It is a powerful irony in life. Uniqueness is far better than cookie-cutter clones. When we can authentically embrace our uniqueness, we become a magnet to others and doors fling open to genuine friendships.

The concept of this unique mindset originated one day when I finally gathered many close friends, poolside for an afternoon to meet each other. They had all heard about one another over the years and I decided it would be easy and fun to mix my inner circle. While I was floating, I overheard them each asking one another how they met me. With a name like Elizabeth, each friend called me a separate nickname, and that made me laugh. Each recounted how they met me, and how surprised they were that I had initiated a friendship. Then they all laughed and said, "Well, that's what she does. Elizabeth "collects her friends."

That statement defined what I have been doing my whole life. It was one of my happiest moments in life realizing how my intentional actions resulted in blending new friends together and along the way I had brought joy into their lives too.

Adopting the intentional mindset of *Collecting True Friends* is introduced in this book, allowing you to push through past friendship disappointments. When adopted, it can provide the beginning of a mindset overhaul for someone lacking real friends. Finally, it can give you a radar to spot amazing people who might be worthy of your time and devotion as loyal friends in the future. All you must do is stay open to what is about to be shared.

Let this book serve as your personal guide on updating your mindset and methods when connecting with others. Your life is so busy. Permit yourself a few extra moments to reflect during the chapters on the Pondering Pause sections included. They are there to provide you an opportunity to digest and absorb the concepts and practical techniques shared.

As you hear the stories and feel the examples' impact, you will refocus your mind and energies on how you see others in your life now and those you meet in the future. The intent of *Collecting True Friend*s is to give you the tools to seek and identify the best friendship opportunities throughout your busy life. Lastly, be kind to yourself because it takes time to become a better version of a friend to others. We were never formally taught in school how to develop a quality inner circle of friends. So, here's your chance to "grab pearls of wisdom" that work. Let's jump in!

CHAPTER 2
WHO IS INSIDE YOUR INNER CIRCLE?

How often have we seen a woman lugging around a heavy purse filled to the brim with who knows what? Carrying around a huge bag is a form of collecting. It can create a sense of comfort when full, just as the crow gathers shiny items for its nest. Some of our girlfriends carry around a treasure trove of wonders in their handbags, yet they seem to struggle to find the item they need. It made me wonder why a woman would tote around collected things even while realizing some fell to the bottom to become forgotten. Was she consciously aware of the added weight as her handbag's contents grew and grew? It didn't just happen overnight. I believe whether or not she realized it, she made a series of decisions. At one time, she picked up an item, regarded its value, decided she might need it, and popped it into what she calls a purse (some may call it baggage). Those items were carefully selected and considered valuable at one time. Some items gave her an immediate sense of comfort by being readily accessible, while others merely contributed to the purse's weight. Why does it take her so long before she will flip it over and dump the contents out on the counter for a review?

Why are we talking about someone filling up their handbag with clutter versus a few items they will need? That is the right question to explore in reflection of the people we frequently see and choose to keep in our inner circle. Just like the oversized purse ballooning, that is how many of our inner circles get filled up over time. An inner circle of friends are the ones who influence you and with whom you share your time, energy, and generosity. Once inside the tight circle, as time passes, few are removed because of history shared. Recognizing who is in your inner circle today is the first step in evaluating if you intentionally included them into your world or they just showed up. Crowding up our inner circle with the wrong people limits the ability and room to collect true friends.

A heavy handbag is like an inner circle full of people that at one time we regarded with interest and invited into our world. Over time, some yielded great joy, wisdom, and love, while others started out making sense in our lives, then eventually just added weight. The ones that weighed us down could be those with values you no longer are willing to accept, whose lives are always full of drama, or seem to enjoy the tension. Seeing more clearly who is in your inner circle and understanding why they landed there will clarify how you should welcome future friendships. It is a fundamental start to understanding what you want now in your life and what steps to take to make great friendships happen.

There is a price to pay when we don't pay attention to who is in our lives. It can cost us more emotionally than the rewards generated. Much like the oversized purse, the friendship becomes heavy to the carrier. Then one day (and we've all been there), we pick it up and grunt, thinking it too heavy to bear. Only at that point do we finally question what we are doing. Things no longer feel right or bring happiness. That is the moment of an awakening when things seem wrong, and we want to find more joy.

An inner circle of friends looks like the growth rings on the inside of a tree. The tightest ring is the inner circle, the one closest to the tree's center. Those are the people with the highest emotional closeness to you. If you visualize the other rings flowing outwards, they are still part of the tree, yet they are not as close to the center. Usually, those rings are wider and contain more people because our time and energy limit our connection depth (or bandwidth) to the number of people active in our lives.

PONDERING PAUSE:

Our inner circle is much like the purse that grew from our conscious choices about what to keep.

- Do my current friends bring out the best in me? *Note: When answering this question, make sure to consider where you are in your current life.*

- Have I kept my same collection of friends around me forever, yet something now feels wrong? Perhaps, I have changed, or they changed.

- Do I find myself feeling drained after talking with certain friends? If yes, I will write down names and consider limiting my exposure for the _____ period. After having some distance, I will assess how much I missed them in my life.

- Are there any other friends I want to be closer to? If yes, I will write down names to reconnect and catch up more frequently.

- After spending time with others who were "not-as-close" friends, I realize I want to see them more frequently. I will write their names, so I remember to reach out. Their names are:

_____.

Gaining Your Inner Circle of Friends—Guard Your Inner Circle

We should regard our inner circle as a precious personal thing that we guard and own. Notice I used the word guard. Why do we hesitate to review them and update who should be in our inner circle of friends? Are we afraid others will think we are mean-spirited by blocking them from getting closer? We were told as kids to "be nice" yet, not provided clear instructions or consequences.

As we age, we are supposed to behave as better human beings, so naturally, a nicety level prevails. Nicety makes us not want to offend anyone. However, not speaking the truth to friends who act like jerks can cause future grief. There is a danger from festering until you've reached your ultimate emotional limit. At that point, it's almost like someone reached over to remove your cork, and BAM outflows the emotions. Sadly, at that point, the result is usually a poorly delivered message to the other person. When you fail to take the time and "dump out your handbag and take a look at what's inside," you can risk being goaded into saying things you wished you had handled differently. Plus, those observing can misinterpret emotional outbursts. They might think you are irrational, not having the history of the events leading up to that intense moment witnessed in your friendship.

Whenever such a time happened to me, I deeply regretted it, wishing I had been more aware of who had gotten too close and been better trained. If only I could stay more logical, more left-brained, like a Vulcan character on a sci-fi show. Instead, I would get emotionally jerked around until I reacted in an unpredictable way, or what I call an "amygdala hijack." So, by learning the skill to speak my truth calmly and with grace is a communication jewel I'd like to share with you so you can protect your inner circle of friends. Even if it's not something you understand in this moment, aim to remember not to let your emotions control what comes out of your mouth to your closest friends. Cool off first if something they do disappoints or distresses you. Then fully process what happened so you can think through how best to react. Sometimes the best action is no action at all.

Sticks and Stones
"Sticks and stones can break my bones, but words can never hurt me." That's a lie. Words can torment and minimize a person or uplift and refocus someone to become a better version of themselves. Within an inner circle of friends are real people with emotions developed over decades of experiences and influence. Keeping and growing an inner circle with the people who can make you a better person and likewise requires honesty in conversations. Those are the people to treasure and ensure they know how deeply you value them. Then, if something ever goes amiss, the right words can diffuse a tense situation. There are meanings in your words, so be aware of how you talk with a friend to

ensure positive results. Conversely, the wrong words can hurt your friend, and your intended message is lost. Something you thought was super important to talk about then never gets addressed. That's a tough place!

You have a big responsibility when speaking your truth because of the power held in words. You also have a responsibility to be brave and NOT chicken out when it's time to talk in a friendship. Choosing the best words will guide you to open the discussion without flinging unnecessary hurt. You don't have to be a writer to pick words that describe a situation carefully. Just search for the right words that relay the feeling behind the message. Instead of saying "I was sad when you didn't show up at the dinner," you could relay, *I wanted us to catch up, and not having you at the dinner was a big disappointment—you were missed!* Can you feel the difference in the message?

Speaking Your Truth in Ways to Protect Your Inner Circle
Having a healthy inner circle of friends is something to be treasured and nurtured. It requires clear communication to get to know each other in deeper and sensible ways for handling disagreements or hurt feelings. Being honest and talking with a dear friend about something they did that aggravated you require clear boundaries. Let's clarify the parameters about being fair or speaking your truth. You can be frank without being blunt. But at the same time, you need to get to the point. Learn to tell your truth while you strive to remember the benefits of using a filter. Choose your words wisely because they carry real power. One word can uplift a soul or crush it. Many a friendship or work relationship has ceased over a single conversation delivered hastily. If someone has an emotional outburst with you, first consider if they have a valid message. You may be in the wrong. Secondly, weigh the information to see if you need to change your behavior in the future. If so, determine how you can correct this situation since you caused unhappiness. Thirdly, remember to apologize if you have hurt your friend. Tell them it was never your intent.

No one enjoys watching someone blast another, and when confronted, the rude person dismisses their rudeness with a blanket excuse of "I'm just keeping it real!" Such people confuse us with what is a cruel jab, but they label it as their truth. They cover it up by saying, "I'm just joking." Being hurtful and wounding to another person is not speaking the truth. It is an attack and a clear sign that a person should not be in your inner circle. If you begin to realize they are jabbing you with "helpful hints" to correct your behavior or mock the things you do, stop right there and evaluate why you are keeping them in your circle of friends. A filter that lets too much through is not a filter, and a filter that allows nothing through blocks your message. Aim to develop using a "practical filter," meaning your message and truth can be said without damaging your friend. Likewise, look within your inner circle to ensure your friends practice the same. Like attracts like. Define and then role-model your expectations for others to express their truths. Encourage your friends to talk with grace and tact to improve each other's lives without hurting another. This is especially important if you decide to introduce your friends to hang out together and then you see it doesn't go well. It is awkward to witness one of your friends disturbed over what another great friend said because she acted cluelessly or failed to listen enough.

It is in your best interest to choose words carefully. Emotions should not solely dictate your vocabulary. Let your words be heartfelt and concise, delivered with pauses to allow your truth to sink in. Profanity or yelling distracts and overshadows your message. Remember, the mouth talks faster than the brain can absorb the news, so speak slower when sharing a crucial conversation. A true friendship grows deeper when both care to learn more and listen to what's important to their friend. Likewise, they must possess the ability to mend hurt feelings that occasionally arise, even in the best friendships.

One of my rural co-workers would softly say to someone acting rude in the office, "You better check yourself before you wreck yourself!" It was directly to the point and highly effective. I loved this non-threatening reminder that made someone reconsider their actions. She always said it with a smile and a wink, which softened the impact.

We've established that our words have real power. Let's talk about the timing of a message to someone in your inner circle. Choosing an optimal time to speak with your friend will aid in a more successful interaction. The ideal time is when emotions are calmest because that allows for active listening. Also, I have noticed it best to pick a time when my friend is rested. Be willing to delay a crucial conversation if you (or they) are too upset or tired.

 TIP:

Even if something has been troubling you, it can be a news flash to your friend or co-worker when you finally speak your truth. I've seen people worry for days about something they said. They were afraid it was hurtful or inappropriate; only to find out later the person they believed was offended hadn't given it a second thought. Sometimes we find that we have misinterpreted the whole situation. We can be our own worst accusers as well as too quick to judge regarding friends and situations. Taking the time to speak with someone in your inner circle shows how important they are to you, deepening the connection. It can also reveal their character and whether you share the same values. If they value your friendship, they will take the time to listen and make sure the issue is peacefully resolved. Conversations have power; aim to listen to your friends when they speak, really lean in, and assess the words they use and how the message lands on your mind and in your heart. Pay attention to their facial movements and body language as they speak. Actively listen to what they say. Those are endearing qualities a true friend will display, and it has been known to accelerate a person to the true friend status.

PONDERING PAUSE:

ARE YOU GOING THROUGH SOME HEARTACHE NOW WHERE YOUR FRIEND AGGRAVATES OR DISAPPOINTS YOU? IF SO, LET'S TAKE A FEW MOMENTS AND DICTATE A NOTE INTO YOUR PHONE (OR WRITE DOWN) THE FOLLOWING:

- Think of words and actions to best describe what happened. I felt
  _____.

- Contrast what occurred to what you had expected to happen.
- How would you like things to be when you see your friend again?

Completing the above Pondering Pause will allow you to think about the change you want to see. Often in friendships or relationships, the upset person hasn't thought enough about what they want to be different. They simply act out. Be determined to know how you want things to be different if such a similar situation arises.

Think it Through – Imagine How You Want the Outcome to Look

Practicing aloud allows you to pause, think it through, and boil it down to a refined message you feel more comfortable delivering. Be sure you close your conversation with what remedy you expect from them (an apology, a fix, a promise not to repeat). Sometimes friends (or co-workers) can hear we are upset, yet they don't know how to get out of the doghouse. Many husbands face this same predicament. If you can shower them with grace and tactfully point out how they can fix their blunder, you have increased the chance for a positive outcome. Can you imagine why showing grace and tact is necessary? There are two reasons. First, it's the right thing to do, and secondly, you might be the goofball one day who has to hear the truth about how you acted poorly. When you are the one who messed up, isn't it better when someone is kind enough to show you how to fix it?

Scroll through the reflections below and be sincere with your answers. If it feels like speaking the truth is a good idea or a necessity to keep the friendship alive, prepare before acting. To prepare, you will have to practice what you plan to say. Your words should be concise and delivered with a clear message. A strategy I find helpful is to rehearse what I plan to say while driving in the car. Hearing myself aloud makes me drop random words and insert planned pauses for clarity. Remember, we speak faster than a human can listen, particularly when we get anxious. So, aim to slow down the delivery of your message. Don't make it personal. Keep to the "when this happened _____, I felt _____." A slower delivery will help the other person fully listen, plus it makes them wonder why you are speaking more deliberately. Raising their curiosity always helps with making sure they listen.

PONDERING PAUSE:

- How important is it to me to speak my truth?
- Does it weigh on my heart and mind **enough** that I want my friend to change something in our friendship?
- Are they capable of change?
  - *If you think they can change, then it's time to speak. If you feel it won't make a difference, save your breath.*
- Am I willing to accept speaking the truth may end our friendship? Is that what's best for me?
- If I decide to speak my truth, which approach would be best for their personality type? How can I tailor my words so they will best hear me?
  - *These examples are some you could consider:*
  - *Do I need a short talk to the point, or a caring nurturer approach?*
  - *Is their communication style too polar to mine so that I can't relate my message? Sometimes opposites don't mix well. Here is an easy assessment tool I use for determining someone's personality. Go to www.MyBankCode.com/Redhawk for a*

quick free personality assessment. Take five minutes to identify your personality type and then try to guess theirs. It should help you craft your conversation tone more thoughtfully.

- Should I accept that sometimes, no matter how hard we try to relate, we will probably not agree? _____Yes _____No
  - *Determining your friend's personality style above is immensely helpful to explain how they will react and guess their potential to change.*

If Only We All Could Man-Talk

Guys are much better at speaking the truth. Guys can call out bad behavior to another guy within their inner circle because they don't embrace the same full range of emotions as women. A man can correct another man's poor behavior, and they don't fester afterward. They say it, move on, and stay friends. The other day, my guy friend had had enough listening to his new co-worker drop the F-bomb during every single paragraph he spoke. Others had noticed too, then distanced themselves. They gave the new guy a temporary grace period to adjust since he transferred from an industry where profanity prevailed. His new world mixed him with female officers and customers, making his colorful language inappropriate and offensive. Man-Talk won the day, and the new guy expressed gratitude for being pulled aside and given feedback. Now the two men are friends.

Most men are better at being discreet when someone has vented to them and direct when dealing with poor behavior. Men quickly determine if they have a dog in the fight and are less likely to jump in unless that person is in their inner circle. Male directness has become condoned as a strength by society. Too much female candor gets women unfairly labeled as bitchy. However, females can save themselves a lot of grief if they learn the art of Man-Talk. When women in the workplace speak their truth positively in a factual, concise, and polished manner, others lean in to listen. In many cases, friendships are forged from the immediate respect generated. I have noticed that I tend to relate quicker to positive women using a Man-Talk style, which deepens a friendship. It is a trait, that when practiced and presented in a heart-felt tone, can make you more of a magnet to potential friends. Why? because your positive message is delivered in a well thought out manner, limiting the time to trigger strong emotions.

We All Have Choices to Make – So Choose Wisely

So back to the story. The new guy at work spouting F-Bombs had choices to make. He had to choose whether to modify his abrasive behavior or ignore the advice given. Plus, he had to decide how he would treat the messenger brave enough to offer advice. Based on his actions, he chose wisely and is now in the inner circle at work. Man-Talk communication mode helps move friendships forward when the person who gave the advice is honored for speaking the truth. The last part is crucial to absorb in this tale. We must honor the person who thought enough of us to take action and give timely feedback so we can become a better version of ourselves.

Nicety Can Hold Women Back from Finding Their Inner Circle

For women, paying more attention to the happiness of others can eventually develop into a value. Women can be more vigilant than men for not wanting to offend, and you'd think that was always a good thing, yet there is a price to be paid. We can stifle our future. Here's a news flash not shared nearly enough with the ladies. Not speaking your truth to your friends and new acquaintances can cripple your efforts to create an abundant world filled with quality friends. It can hold you back from a promotion, hitting personal goals, or becoming the best version of YOU.

Notice I said you can create an abundant world of friends. This blessing can happen starting today. I'm going to call them "quality" friends. What we want more of in our lives are people to enrich our world; those are people with great qualities. Here are questions to consider: Could blindly focusing our energies on being a good person, making friends, thinking of others, and making the world a better place hurt our future in any way? Isn't this what they taught us to do in school: "Get along and be nice to everyone?" Yes, that is what we were told. However, it was a proclamation given without any set of directions or guidelines to follow. Consequently, good intentions and energies can sometimes land on barren fields.

Here is the conflict that can happen when we blindly follow the whole "be nice and get along with others" standard. We likewise expect others will get along and be nice to us. With all the bullying I endured as the *Little Viking Girl*, you'd think that would have been more obvious to me. So, here is the truth. Sometimes no matter how hard you try to be friendly; some people still won't like you. And that is alright. That's how life works, yet many of us, including me, were unaware of this fact for most of our early years.

By always putting others first and blindly giving unconditionally, you become a magnet for lesser quality people. This scenario happened to me in my twenties. I allowed some unworthy people to mix into my inner circle of quality friends. Time and time again, I jumped in as the rescuer and failed to see they had no genuine desire to improve. Finally, I realized I wanted more for them than they did for themselves. Not paying enough attention to who got into my inner circle cost me years of frustration and confusion. I foolishly thought I was there to help constantly uplift them. Only later did I understand where my excessive good intentions originated from. I am a child of an alcoholic. Such a background can mold a person into that reliable person willing to race in to fix everyone's problems. I would apply my strategic mind and tenacity to enlist the needed resources and voila, problem solved! I got so good at helping others; I believed I could fix anything and anyone if only I just tried harder. Those who resisted would eventually get energized and succeed, just like me. I wanted nothing from them, just everything for them. I simply wanted them to be and feel blessed like I did. However, when this happens, the wrong people get too close. What

I learned is I pleased people in my inner circle who were not worthy of my time and devotion. Ultimately, giving too much of myself caused a significant health issue, and I lost all my energy. Overnight I went from being the supercharged overachiever saving the world to feeling like a helpless lump. That is a cost anyone can pay when not guarding their inner circle.

So now let's answer the question we started with. "Could blindly focusing your energies on being a good person cause damage?" The answer is yes. Because without setting an intention and design of who we want to attract, it opens our world to confusion over whom to pursue as friends. If we don't know what we want more of in our lives, how will we ever recognize it when standing in front of us? Well then, what does work? First, it is best to create a place in your heart to explore and understand what a true friend means to you and compile those qualities onto a list. This can be refreshing or surprising when you see what qualities you value in friendship. Either way, it opens your mind to awareness. This very important step will be repeated throughout the book, so please make sure you take the time to create this qualities list. It will become your foundational checklist in your journey to Collect True Friends. Think of that list as a reflection pool to help clarify and remember the types of friends you desire in life. I discuss this topic in depth in Chapter 4, Inventory Check.

R-E-S-P-E-C-T is Not Just a Great Song
When looking to accept new friendships, there are some truths to realize. What school didn't clearly explain, or prepare us for in the real world, is that not everyone gets along with everyone. Sometimes, no matter what we do, we will never like that person or likewise. Instead of blindly helping and liking others, we should have learned more about respecting others and tolerating their differences. It is ok not to like everyone we meet, and vice versa. We must, however, treat others with respect and grace and accept one another.

Here are some things I observed and learned in my quest that helped me better understand how to develop friendships:

- Real friendships are earned.
- Real friendships earned are to be valued.
- Real friendships happen when you are both worthy.
- Real friendships help each other personally develop.
- Everyone should respect everyone.
- Not everyone will make a great friend for you.
- Some people should always stay on the outside of your circle.
- Not everyone gets invited into your inner circle.
- You may not get invited into someone's inner circle. It is their choice.
- Some inner circles take longer to enter because the trust and timing are not quite right.
- Trying to be a nice person universally is not the same as being friends with everyone.

 PONDERING PAUSE – TAKE ACTION:

Instructions:

Grab a pen and paper or a device to answer the following questions. You might find it helpful to include friends for clarity, but that is optional. When completed, put away your list of answers for the day. Look at it daily for the next seven days to notice how your heart feels when reviewing the answers and the friend's name(s).

- Which of my friends do I wish would use a filter more?
- Does that friend say what they feel regardless of how it could hurt another?
- Which friend do I appreciate because they can Man-Talk?
- Do I have a friend that talks a lot yet says nothing?
- How would my inner circle friends rate my ability to listen enough? ____1 poor to 10 terrific

- How would my friends describe my ability to communicate (speak my truth)?
- Which friend(s) do I learn new things from?
- Do I believe I make my friends proud? Do they proudly say we are friends?
- How many of my friends introduce me to their inner circle of friends?
- Of my inner circle friends, which friend(s) considers me part of their inner circle?

We've explored the power of having an inner circle of friends, worthy of your time and devotion and why you must work to guard it. Helpful tools for meaningful conversation with those in your inner circles were shared. Plus, how to handle awkward moments in a friendship by using Man-Talk and Speaking Your Truth. The Pondering Pause sections helped assess your current friendships levels regarding their individual value. Recognizing how significant they are in your life will add clarity on what energy levels you should dedicate. You are doing great, and it is now time to grab your Pondering Pause answers and move onto Chapter 3 for further clarity. We will discover "Who Gets Invited Inside Your Inner Circle?" and why.

CHAPTER 3
YOUR INNER CIRCLE – WHO GETS INVITED?
How To Best Grow the Circle?
Assess Who Needs to Leave?

Your Journey Begins

Practicing the art of "collecting true friends" requires a layered learning approach. Imagine opening your world to friendship opportunities as a stairway you climb one step at a time. *Embracing this new concept of collecting true friends* was your first big step. Well done! Learning this concept and applying it might seem daunting at first. It might appear more like ascending the steep stone steps of a Mayan pyramid rather than a flight of house stairs. Some steps may feel taller than others. That's because this process will push you out of your comfort zone. That's ok. Once you get to the top of the stairs, the view is magnificent, and that is where great things happen because you stayed the course.

Don't fret if this journey to opening friendships feels awkward at times. As we continue, you will learn step-by-step what you need, so your journey makes sense and feels easier. There is no rush to the top. Commitment and determination will help you reach it. Start by reminding yourself of the world you want to create. One that is filled with enriching friendships. Now pretend you took a journey towards your greatness. Sit still for the next two minutes and try a quick exercise. I find this visualization technique incredibly helpful when preparing to tackle something new.

Close your eyes. Visualize yourself walking to the stairway, see the landing way at the top. Begin to climb the stairs—step-by-step. Midway up, stop to feel the sun on your face, and you take a deep breath. Continue lifting each leg and climbing until you are almost there. You can see the last step. At the very top is a collection of true friends who've been waiting to meet you. They are now visible. When you take your final step, they grab your hand and pull you up to the landing. They loudly rejoice that YOU kept climbing to reach them. It was well worth the climb!

Now take ten more seconds and reflect on how you felt when reaching the top and hearing them rejoice. How did that feel in your heart? Did it give you a boost of confidence or more energy for the journey? Tell yourself that doubt has no seat on your trip because you are the driver of change, and you will become a magnet for genuine friendships.

If you still feel apprehensive about climbing the steps to your new world of friendships, try this pacifier technique to calm any emotional charges. Cup your hand on the lower back of your head, near the neck. Feel the warmth exchanged. Hold it there, take a deep breath. Try to permit it to calm you, pacifying any fear of trying to bubble. While cupping your hand above your back neck, repeat the same climbing stairs visualization exercise. See yourself climb those stairs bottom to the top until you finally meet the new friends who've been patiently awaiting your arrival. If at any time doubt tries to creep back into your mind or heart, repeat that exercise and tell doubt it serves no purpose on this journey. Dovetail this page so you can quickly come right back here to do this visualization. Think of it as your reset button.

Moving forward, let's examine what else we've covered. Adopting and *keeping an open mindset to act deliberately* when viewing who's inside your inner circle of friends (or not) was your second step. We learned it is necessary to become more aware of those in our current lives, speak our truth in ways healthy for friendships, and assess how we feel. That was a big second step towards gaining your awareness of who's in your current circle of friends.

Step 1 Adopt the concept of *Collecting True Friends.*
Step 2 Open the mind to act deliberately.
Step 3 Be Truthful about the people around you.

Time to move onto Step 3: Let's peek at the *quality* of people inside your inner circle right now. It requires being truthful with yourself about who surrounds you. Ask yourself these questions aloud for a baseline:

- Do my friends make me a better person?
- Which friend(s) lacks qualities I feel are essential in a true friend?
- Who do I want to spend more time with?
- Who do I not miss when unseen for a while?

It requires some time to "vet" someone's values and qualities, but there is good news. The risk of adding drama to your world is significantly reduced when we first study someone's values and qualities. It is a peek into their soul and what makes them tick. Your goal is to determine if their qualities, traits, and values align with yours. A clever way to do this is by applying the powerful tools of awareness and discernment we've been discussing.

A Past Life That Has Lacked True Friends is Fixable!
There is hope we are all capable of adding better friends to our life. An abundance of excellent friends is achievable over time. What you must ensure is to model qualities that attract the best people. Meaning like attracts like. If there is something you are doing that is a negative behavior, it is a great time to make a conscious effort to break that habit. Prayer is a great healer to cease behaviors that don't serve us or cause harm to another. For example, I was a constant worrier. I wasn't very good at worrying because the things I concentrated on never were future problems. It seemed like I was always trying to predict and be prepared for what could happen. That was not only a realistic behavior, but it was exhausting. Plus, it made me less appealing to others because I would overcompensate in preparations, thinking I could make all things perfect.

When I finally realized Worry was draining my life, I made a choice. From that moment, I would be more conscious of that negative trait and ask my inner circle to help me look for ways to reduce the Worry. I could not tackle it alone and needed help. I was praying to possess a feeling of certainty that all would be well, so I could feel calmer. My prayer of deliverance finally took root, and with practice, I did find relief from the chains of Worry. It required making a conscious effort to no longer feed the harmful habit of Worry. Likewise, asking my friends to help me spot when that negative behavior surfaced helped me curtail its intensity. Occasionally, I worry, but now I am aware it is an energy-sucking emotion. Sometimes it tries to creep into my thoughts, and I have to say aloud, "Worry, go away! Quit clouding my judgment."

You may ask, "How can a negative emotion or habit really be detrimental to collecting true friends?" Let's use my example when I acted as an extreme worrier. People were uncomfortable being around such a person because of the vibes they feel. It confused them. They saw a confident smiling person but also felt something else intense. They sensed the presence of an anxious energy, which can feel contagious. Here is a truth bomb. Finding potential friends requires that we possess more positive emotions than negative emotions. Social health studies show that increasing our levels of positivity makes us appear more appealing to others. Recently I learned that Worry itself is rooted in fear and acts like a bondage harming the soul. A bondage is something that attaches itself to a person's life. In small doses, it can be acceptable to keep us alert, but in great quantities or repeatedly practiced, it becomes an addiction. Much like a bit of caffeine can give us pleasure, but seven cups a day is unhealthy.

 PONDERING PAUSE:

- Can you name a negative trait you possess that makes others feel uncomfortable?

- Could you commit to reducing or eliminating that personality trait? *Not only will you feel better you will also become more of a magnet to amazing friends.*
- Can you pray (or meditate) for permanent liberation from that negative emotion?
- Can you identify a trusted friend to share your goal to eliminate that named negative emotion? Ask them to remind you if it presents again.

In Friendships, Quality Over Quantity Always Wins

There are more opportunities for friendships worthy of your time and devotion when you welcome others with extraordinary qualities regardless if they blend in with your inner circle. In friendships, quality is better than quantity. Grab the richness of life by expanding your current thinking about who you find interesting. In the future, some of your best friends may not be a cookie-cutter version of yourself. When searching instead for specific qualities and traits in others, you notice you desire quality friends over quantity of friends.

Have you ever been in a large group or party and yet felt disconnected from the people? That can happen when we are not where we are supposed to be. Many times, it is our cue to exit because those people are not our tribe. They might have been at one time. However, feeling disconnected can also mean those are not the people who can become your true friends. That is for you to consider carefully and your call to make after assessing. It is possible that sometimes we haven't spent enough time in the group to assimilate, but usually, it simply means we don't fit in there. If that is the answer you arrive at, that is alright.

Physical attributes can be deceiving. What lies underneath is a person's true character. So, here's the question to ask yourself: "If I can't accurately read people by appearance, how can I best determine if they are a fit in my inner circle?" The answer is by learning the person's qualities and values. Those two things should determine how to see them and if they warrant an invitation to know you better.

My open-mindedness grew from being the *Little Viking Girl* who never blended into a large group. What started as a necessity to assimilate later grew into being thankful to those who were warm and genuine. Their goodness was a quality I could sense instead of assessing them solely by their appearance.

Let's explore how we use a lens to assess others' authentic characters and determine what traits they possess. Hopefully, you are now more open to consider a wider variety of friendships. Such a mixture of friends opens the mind to new concepts, customs, struggles, and dreams. It will make you appear more interesting (like a magnet) to others because you become more worldly, accepting how different God made us all. It also educates us about who we are, where we come from, and where we want to go. A greater variety of friends will push you to learn constantly, and suddenly the world does not seem so big. For example, hearing my international friends talk about their beautiful homelands and foods created my desire to travel to new lands. Being around more believers broadened my faith by hearing their stories about how they served using their talents.

A Brief Note About My Belief in God

Decades ago, I saw a film clip about a four-year-old child who could not walk. The child would stand up, take one step and fall. The therapist attached a rope to the ceiling and let the child hold the rope while taking a few steps. The child could walk without falling. When the therapist took the rope away, the child would take a step and fall. It continued this way, month after month, but the therapist noticed something. Sometimes the rope was slack. So, the therapist held a short length of rope for the child to hold on to, and when the child started walking, the therapist let go of the rope. The child walked all around the room with his hand in the air, holding a small limp piece of rope.

Maybe you believe God takes an active role in your life. I certainly do. Maybe you question if God is real, and you succeed on your own. I don't think God minds either way. Your success is what matters.

After all, did the rope help the child walk or not?

Sometimes you may not feel you've done enough in life, or your life is off track for your age. When you feel those emotions of uncertainty bubble up, that is a great time to compare your world to a friend's, to bring clarity for both of you. Seeing another's lifestyle sometimes reminds us of a former dream forgotten or a difficult time we luckily conquered. Our memories can fade the struggles we survived or sadly erase something we once dreamt of achieving. Even though I have hit some big goals, sometimes I forgot how hard the struggle was until I relived a memory after hearing a new friend share the same challenge. You'd be surprised how being vulnerable and sharing your past can inspire a friend to pursue her/his big goals. From your openness, friends discover how you too struggled yet reached success. Many times, others see who we are today and think success magically falls into our hands. Great friendships can blossom when you take the time to be transparent about your journey and offer to help those on the same paths.

Know, Like, Trust, and be Memorable (in a Good Way)
Four essential levels exist that you must recognize when getting acquainted with a person better: know, like, trust, and be memorable. Learning these four levels will accelerate your ability to become a magnet to others. Think of these as great tools you pull out as you approach an acquaintance or friend. Research says we have seven seconds to make a good initial impression. If you only have one opportunity to make a good impression, and it can make or ruin a career or budding relationship, why not use methods that succeed!

Proceed and succeed following this order: People have to know, like, trust, and remember you. Here is a news flash on being memorable; your goal is to be memorable in a good way! I have met people who were quite memorable, meaning I will NEVER forget them because of what they said or how poorly they acted. Nobody wants to be remembered in that way!

Be Memorable in A Good Way

Here are some of my proven tips:

- Try to find a way to make yourself helpful. For example, stop and hold the door for someone carrying boxes.
- Be gracious if something is not going well. Never be rude or criticize. Act in ways a true friend should act even though you've just met the person.
- If you overhear someone searching for something that you have or are trained in, offer to share some input, or lend a tool.
- Offer to introduce others. If you've met a fellow enthusiast, introduce her to your good friend and explain they share a mutual interest (i.e., horseback riding or hiking).
- Support the person's passion, business, charity, or project, either by volunteering or donating. Or you could find them a volunteer or resource they need. Or you could find them a volunteer or resource they need. For example, you buy something that they are selling, even if you don't personally need it. You can buy it and give it to another friend.
- Be a delightful guest. Be gracious and inclusive of others. Leave others around you feeling glad they met you. Bring a token gift when invited to a home.
- Show gratitude. Send a card showing your appreciation or a note to say it was nice to meet them.
- Listen well to what they say. Remember the details of their stories and make a mental note of key things in their life. When you see them again, ask how those things are going.

- If in doubt about how best to act during an awkward situation, be a role model of elegance. You may not have all the facts, so it is best to take the "high road."
- Make an effort to connect genuinely to everyone— not just those who may be of value or interesting to you.

As we've been exploring who gets invited into your inner circle, it is important to understand what you want more of in your life. The goal is to be magnetic to what you desire and what's mutually uplifting for both of you. So here are some things to consider. What characteristics attract others to you, and what characteristics attract you to others? It is key to know and declare. For example, I am drawn to those displaying kindness, curiosity, and a willingness to learn.

Here is my list of the main qualities I seek from potential friends. I look for people who make me:

- think
- laugh
- confident
- learn
- strong
- devout
- brave
- grow
- healthy
- explore
- happy

- love
- strategize
- understand
- dream
- nurture
- plan
- ponder
- focus
- play
- try
- explore

Now it is your turn; think and say your answer to this question: "I look for people who make me_____."

PONDERING PAUSE:

About Your Inner Circle – Grab your paper or device to reflect and answer the following:

- The qualities (traits) I like most in friends are _____
- My inner circle is filled with friends possessing those traits:
  __Yes __No __ Somewhat
- I want more people with these traits _____, _____, _____
  as close friends.
- The qualities (traits) most missing amongst my friends in my current inner circle are _____.
- My friends all think and talk alike (their values agree most of the time). ___Yes ___No
- My inner circle of friends encourages personal growth.
  ___Yes ___No ___Hardly
- Are my friends varied in looks and backgrounds?
  ___Yes ___No ___ Somewhat
- Have I become a better person by mixing with my current group of friends? __Yes __No __ Unsure

Reading your answers above will help you filter out what is missing in your life regarding the type of friends you have attracted or pursued. Now, let's drill that down a little bit deeper to analyze your thoughts so you can prepare to attract more specific friendships.

EXERCISE

Referencing your above answers, open a blank page to start a new list for intently growing your inner circle.
Draw three columns.
Label the first column QUALITIES TO ATTRACT.
Label the second column LIKELY FRIEND.
Label the third column ACQUAINTANCE

- List the qualities in a friend you want to attract into your inner circle in column one.
- Write the names of anyone who pops into your mind possessing those qualities. Think (or pray) with discernment while reviewing your potential friends in column two or three.
- As you meet others in the future, look back at your qualities list and ask yourself if that person displays any of those traits you seek more of in your inner circle. If so, add their name to column two or three.

HERE IS A SAMPLE GRAPH:

GROWING YOUR INNER CIRCLE

Qualities to Attract	Likely Friend	Acquaintance
friendly		Lynn
curious	Melinda	
strong		
devout	Laurie	Jerome
dreams		Jeff
grows	Lakeisha	
healthy		Vikki
explores	Debbie	
happy		
loving	Kate	
playful	Karin	
travels		Michael
smart/thinks	Andrea	
entrepreneur		Connie
goal focused	Jackie	

Create A Mental Checklist – Discernment Guides Growth in Your Circle

Why is using discernment about whom you invite into your circle vital to your happiness? As we age, society expects us to become wiser. Since wisdom is experience combined with knowledge, the goal is to never repeat the same mistake. When we only gain more experience, yet not enough knowledge, we fail to gain wisdom. That's where discernment jumps in like a superpower you can use every day. It is the ability to distinguish between things based on prior knowledge and experiences. I think of discernment as a quality that, when gained, can help us all grasp and comprehend what is not apparent when building relationships. When you write out your values, it creates mental awareness and discernment is allowed to grow. I like to consult my values when deciding who gets invited into my inner circle. Why do I recommend you do that as well? Because knowing what is dear to you in friendships, or a career relationship, will make it much easier to attract the right people into your space.

Checklist if Values Align with a Potential Friend

Creating yourself a mental list or checklist tool can greatly help you react with clarity after meeting others. Awareness kicks in like a backup generator when you are talking with someone new. You become determined to spot the important values, qualities, and characteristics to pay attention to. I highly recommend you take the time to create your mental checklist. Training yourself is a huge timesaver in relationship building. It's like an internal dashboard that helps signal how things are functioning when engaging with someone you haven't known long enough.

A mental checklist is activated using awareness and discernment. When both are consistently applied and eventually mastered, your journey to find new friends feels lighter. That's when the fun begins. Ultimately, growing your inner circle can be more enjoyable because you start to see the results. You begin making wonderful friendships with those who align with your values.

Let me show you how it works. If you don't have a mental awareness list, you can start with my list. <u>Instructions</u>: Before I invite an acquaintance out again, or make it known I want to be better friends, or bring them into my inner circle, I consult this mental checklist. Over time, I observe or discover information about that potential friend. Such things I would seek to know are as follows:

- Who else (that I like) knows and trusts the person?
- What makes her laugh or feel passionate?
- Have I noticed how well he mixed with others at different events or work occasions?
- Have I witnessed how she interacted with the public?
  - Notice their manners when speaking with staff and servers.
- Did I listen enough to get a deep sense of how they think or did I do all the sharing?
- Is she discrete with information or is she a gossip?
- What things do we both enjoy?
- Are there any obvious bad habits?
- Did I pick up on their noticeable likes and dislikes?
  - Am I alright with what they do not like? (i.e., politics, animals, etc.)
- Am I comfortable with their content on their social media posts?
- Which values do we both share?
- What would I like to learn more about them?
- What do I admire about them?
- Do they have a hobby I'd like to try?
- Are they usually on time or arrive rushed and frazzled when seeing others?
- Did they mention reciprocal hosting?
- If their thoughts and interests differ from mine, are they still healthy for me?

- Are they self-centered or genuinely interested in others?
- Can I spot a non-negotiable that would make me reconsider befriending that person? (For example, I attract godly people and shun evil).
- Energy check: After we catch-up, do I feel positive, or does my energy feel icky?

Be Careful Who You Hang Out With

Family, colleagues, friends, and acquaintances influence our outlook on life. We should be learning from those around us and making better decisions. Our inner circle has a tremendous influence on our behavior. Remember when your mom used to say, "Be careful who you hang out with. It affects your reputation." She was right. It also attracts or repels those who want to become your friends. Are you grasping that logic? It means if your inner circle is full of negative people who hate change, they will want you to stay the same, and you will be locked into the world they define. Here is a truth bomb. Where you are now is where you shall stay.

When learned, awareness *plus discernment* will allow you to read the real characters of others more accurately. You will assess situations with greater clarity and not allow drama or hot messes to thrive near you. Won't it feel better in the future to have friends who bless your world instead of wishing you'd never met?

Practice Discernment Like a Superpower

Be patient as you learn to become more mindful when observing others. It takes practice to become skilled in applying discernment when meeting and mixing with others. My big heart can still cloud my good judgment because I try to find the good in everyone. Sometimes I get fooled. I call those people POSERS or TAKERS. Remember when we were little, and there was always that kid that said she could do something better than us? A real braggart who made others believe they did everything right while not doing it. They were a cool imposter, pretending they were the real deal. That's a Poser. They love to take the energy, time, and affection of others. They are void of empathy, compassion, or any depth of emotion for others in need. Some may call it narcissism. They do not contribute to a friend's well-being.

A Poser/Taker connects for their needs and fools others into thinking they are essential. You can spot them because they frequently show up when convenient for them or their plans. They can be so smooth-talking that we overlook how self-absorbed they are, and we naively allow them into our inner circle. We tell them all sorts of things about ourselves or the past because we think it is safe to confide. They may be good-looking or charming or arrive at an opportune time for them when we are vulnerable, needing help. They are so skilled at being likable, it can cloud our ability to see what they love the most, which is themselves. So how can your awareness and discernment alert you? There is usually drama or strife that gives you the first clue this person attracts the opposite of what you desire in friendships. The second clue is it usually repeats. Posers and Takers should never be your first choice to call in a life crisis. They might be family, friends, co-workers, or a potential friend. When you continuously apply social discernment and spot such a person, you will remember NEVER to count on them. That Poser or Taker won't be your go-to person and the great news is you won't be left hanging.

Here is a litmus test to determine if red flags indicate that a higher level of discernment is appropriate for a certain person.
- Have they repeatedly disappointed you with their actions?
- Have their actions caused you to wince or feel embarrassed?
- Have they consistently failed to fulfill what they promised?

A wise man once taught me to never expect more from someone than they are capable of; that way, you don't get disappointed. I married that wise man.

We've covered some of the top qualities that can make us attractive as friends, plus the vital need to practice social discernment when seeing others.

 PONDERING PAUSE:

- Is there someone in my life right now that could be a poser or taker?
- Has that person continued to let me down when I needed help?
- Are they truly capable of being there for me in the future?
- Did I try to "speak my truth" (covered in Chapter 2) on how that made me feel?
- Do they now know how I want our friendship to be different?
- Is it now time to apply the final discernment question: "Should that person stay close in my inner circle of friends?"
  ___ Yes ___No ___ Need to think on it

Your Ability for Growing Your Inner Circle of Friends

Actively connecting is what makes and keeps someone part of your inner circle. The exception to this rule is a treasured long-time friend. Neither time nor distance can dilute such a friendship. Hopefully, you have had the honor and pleasure to have one of those in your life. Life can get in the way, and you will always be dear friends. It can feel like forever since you've talked, and then the moment you hear each other's voices, you pick up where you left off. My dear friend Martha calls this your "2:00 a.m. friend," meaning, the person you can call any time of the day or night. Grab your list and write down who your 2:00 a.m. friend is. Another of my friends calls this your "bail money without judgment, friend."

Energy for Expanding Your Inner Circle – What's Your Capacity?

Before we talk about who gets to stay in your friendship circle, understand there are some essential requirements to keep that circle of friendship happening. Let's talk briefly about the energy required to sustain a friendship. Additional friends require energy plus time on our busy calendars. Weaving new people into your inner circle to share fresh ideas is a healthy goal. Those with fresh thoughts foster personal growth, plus you can reciprocate by sharing your talents and wisdom. Yet to open your circle to include additional friends means you also have to make room in your life. According to the Dunbar Study, we can maintain 150+ recognized relationships in our lives. If you are an introvert, that number could seem daunting. Keep in mind that number is over a lifetime. It includes your family and friends; knowing your capacity to create a larger circle of friendships is helpful.

Now, you are probably wondering when we will address who gets to STAY in your circle. You didn't jump right into that because you first needed to see what your current circle looks and feels like. You analyzed that to reveal the qualities you need more of in your future friends. So, before you can invite others to get closer in your world, you have to make sure you are ready to welcome another connection. To grow your inner circle requires commitment and some energy.

Crickets or Ghosting Causes Angst
Nothing is worse than when two people get to know one another, they talk about things to do next time, and then it's crickets! Crickets are the metaphor I use. It means when you are out in a field alone, and the only sound you hear is crickets chirping. There are no calls or follow-ups from your new friend. Nor do you get any communications explaining why they vanished. Some call that ghosting. Sometimes this happens because one person did not reserve any time in their schedule to follow-up with their new friend. I recently observed an example of how confusing this can be on a Facebook post. Someone posted to their friend, "Thanks for wishing me Happy Birthday. I thought I had done something wrong because the last time we met for dinner, you never called again. It's been a year now." Our brains interpret being ignored as being punished for making a mistake. An unexplained absence can be

interpreted differently based on the level of friendship. Sadly, in a new friendship, an absence may be considered an intentional end. In an established friendship, an unexplained absence may be a pause to deal with a life challenge. That is the advantage of building and sharing an emotional bond.

Some social researchers think our minds can only allow emotional closeness up to a finite amount of people, of which only a dozen or fewer get to be in your inner circle. Some people can handle a higher number of friends, and others are more content with a small set of quality friends. I believe that with modern technology, we can maintain a wider reach than in past decades.

We only have so much capacity, or what businesses call bandwidth. That is why it is essential to be aware of who is getting your energy and time. Now is an excellent time to talk about the possibility that not everyone in your current collection of friends is still a good fit. A few may no longer be worthy of your time and devotion. They might require more energy and time than you can provide. Perhaps you used to meet regularly, and now that is impossible, yet they need that frequency to feel connected. Or maybe you might have changed in your values or interests, and they consider your energy no longer a good fit in their world. In this case, an absence from their side could indicate an intentional end.

So why does allocating your time and energy-matter of growing your circle of friends? It becomes a time balance equation. You must make time to socialize with new friends while still having time to nurture your existing circle. As we discussed, new friendships need extra attention, so it does not confuse them if you haven't reached out frequently enough. Growing our circle requires conscious effort to schedule times to develop new friendships while not ignoring your closest friends.

Here is the good news! When the right people are in your lives, it won't feel like work and drain your energy. Studies show the less something feels like work to a person, the higher their energy remains. It is possible to increase the number in your circle of friends and it brings you less drama and more happiness. How is that possible? When you become a magnet that collects true friends, it expedites bonding and trust. You understand them and they understand you. The familiarity and trust allow you genuinely to show up, relax more, and be more spontaneous.

Your bandwidth for expanding your inner circle is like a company adding new products and projects. To do so, they will consider how much they can support the expansion operations. Support means time and resources. In this case, your energy is the resource required to be a worthy friend.

Being a true friend, requires energy to:
- Follow-up with your friend.
- Be fully present when spending time together.
- Plan activities.
- Remember if they find something important, recognize it has value.
- Learn about their likes and dislikes.
- Remember important events or dates.
- Be a friend worthy of having.
- Uplift and bring out the best in your friend (not hold them back).

Decide how much energy you have and are willing to dedicate to develop and keep a larger group of true friends. Friends who remain a good fit in life usually require less energy since patterns and understandings exist. Most friendships endure the test of time when both evolve, supporting complimentary values over the years. There is a profound positive effect that comes from uplifting another's life. That's the beautiful part about growing old with trusted friends and their families. God brings people together that should meet. As friends, what we do to preserve that relationship's longevity stems from our choices and actions taken over the years.

Recapping Your Journey So Far

We kicked off your journey to gain friendships worthy of your time and devotion by identifying ways to become a magnet to fantastic friends. We've looked at how to observe others with a lens to help avoid misunderstandings. We discussed the necessity to quit expecting more from others than they are capable of. We do this to better embrace those with the qualities we need and value. We self-assessed any emotional traits holding us back from connecting well with others. We discussed the power of saying prayers that ask for liberation to deliver us from burdensome emotions (i.e., Worry). We set the intent to reduce negative emotions not serving us, to become more of a magnet to potential friends. Think back to the image of your new friends standing on the top of the stairs awaiting your arrival. We are working on removing anything that slows your ascension to the top.

You can now realize the importance of paying attention to whom you spend time with since it affects your happiness. We define true friends as those who share a common ability to bring out the better version of ourselves. Likewise, we discovered the superpower of discernment when applied as a guiding tool within your current inner circle. You developed a helpful list of traits and qualities to use as an eye-opener showing what you desire in your true friends. You started to create a mental list of what qualities you observe or feel absent in your current circle.

Who Gets Invited into Your Inner Circle?

Surrounding yourself with an abundant number of amazing friendships can be one of life's most significant accomplishments. Consequently, it is essential to choose wisely and not get distracted when inviting people to be closer to you and your friends. You've completed the process of charting out which traits your current friends possess and identifying what qualities or characteristics are missing. So now is the time to reflect.

There may already be someone nearby that would be an ideal true friend, but you have not noticed. Look at your list of ideal qualities to consider if you've met someone possessing those desired traits. Start writing those names down as potential friends. Gathering that information will help you expand your inner circle with those additional types of people to enrich your life. We will explore in Chapter 4 what's in your inventory of friends and the unique people missing in your inner circle. We will continue with this journey together, step-by-step, in the following chapters as you practice these new concepts and techniques to collect true friends.

CHAPTER 4

INVENTORY CHECK FOR HOLES IN YOUR INNER CIRCLE

Who is in your inner circle? What do you need more of?
What do you need less of?

What do you have in your kitchen pantry? I bet the shelves display a colorful selection of daily essentials, specialty items (for baking maybe?), things you have no use for but "they're still good," and some expired items hiding in the back. Now think about your current set of friends as a pantry. What are the proportions of essential friends in the other categories? Do you have a large stock of similar friends or a high mix of unique people? Are you surprised to realize you have several "I have no clue why they are there" friends? Our lives can be so busy that we push things to the back of our "pantry." Things that are new, or we use often, tend to be up front. Behind them are things you use now and then, and behind that . . . who knows?

Consider writing up an inventory of your current friends and next to their name list their skills, talents, hobbies, and goals. Do you have a wide variety or a recurring theme? It is said that "Variety is the spice of life." You may discover that you need to add some spices to your pantry.

These are some examples of the wide variety of friendships I have collected over the years. Seeing this variety might visually trigger some "aha" moments in how you see others near you. I have a Turkish friend who is an amazing cook, a friend who is a brilliant public speaker, another who is a media expert, a jewelry designer, lawyer, boating friends, and equestrian friends. My eclectic mix of friends also includes a Cuban girlfriend who owns a food truck, many business owners, healthcare workers, busy moms, a Kenyan computer wizard, and tradespeople. Various ages, accents, financial levels, physical abilities, and religious backgrounds are represented as well. Why not? I can have the whole world in a backyard cookout.

Surrounding yourself with "like thinkers" or "cookie cutter" personalities creates a "group-think" mentality within our inner circle. Little personal development can take place when no one ever introduces new concepts or motivations into your world. The friends who fit well into our lives ten years ago may or may not be the friends who make your life better today.

If all your friends are single, you might want to add some married couples. They are sure to have experiences that differ from their unmarried friends. If you are single, there is something there for you to learn. If you are married, you have that in common. If all your friends are married, you might want to add some single friends. Playing matchmaker can be challenging, but it can be rewarding too. More on that later.

A good potential friend should have exceptional talents not typical of your current inner circle. Let's take a few moments and consider how widening your inner circle with a few of these experts might enrich your life. You should also consider how including these people in your circle might enrich their lives. Friendship must work both ways.

Here are a few descriptors to categorize friends:

- Artist
- Author
- Culinary expert/baker
- Career-minded professionals
- Mentor
- Opposite sex co-worker
- Volunteer
- Golfer
- Financially astute
- Travel guru
- Prayer Warrior
- Healthy couple-friends
- Health & Nutrition
- Exercise Champion
- Sports Enthusiast
- Fisher/Boater

This is not an exhaustive list, just a starting point. You should add as many descriptors as you need to describe the people currently in your inner circle. Then create a column of other types you are interested in collecting as friends. Contrast your inner circle to discover what is missing in your inventory of friends. That is vital, so you bring awareness to the types of people you want to attract into your life and dedicate time to find them. For example, if you want to learn more about nutrition and fun ways to exercise, those become a targeted audience to meet. I wanted to meet friends who loved to watch football, so I'd have companions in the Autumn season who shared that passion. Wearing my "Cowboys" jersey drew those enthusiastic fans closer to me for a conversation. Even though they might cheer for another team, common interests attract. Now we receive annual invitations to attend games and parties. It all started with being aware and making my interest obvious to others.

The list of possible types you might be interested in attracting into your world is just a start. You first have to reflect and develop your own tailored list. Those were some suggestions to help you imagine the variety and unique value your inner circle could have. Let's take a few moments to discuss in detail how some of these types could bring you joy by exposing you to new ideas and information.

Health, Nutrition, Exercise Champion – always helpful to know someone who is healthier or lives a more active lifestyle than you do because they stay current on the latest trends. They invite you to social fundraisers with other athletic minded, healthy people. They are usually a very positive minded group because of all the endorphins.

Sports Enthusiast – Golfer, Fisher, Boater – they teach us how to relax and have fun doing outdoor activities in nature. They get us out of our comfort zones and onto the waterways, forests, or fields to try new things.

Artists – they bring the creativity and bold expression of exploration in all they see and introduce us to going to museums or meeting others who may be designing or inventing new things.

Culinary expert, baker – They love food and so do I! They show us a whole new world watching them cook or bake. These experts elevate cooking to a science and art. Their excitement and passion are contagious and open our eyes to new spices, methods, recipes, and cultures. Since I am a huge foodie, I love these types of friends because as a bonus I get to eat delicious new meals!

Career-minded Professionals & Entrepreneurs – These are the driven people that love to share where they are going next and help us in our jobs and careers. Their ambition motivates us to move forward, being financially sound, and making plans for the future. If you want to learn how to be successful, hang out with successful people.

Mentors – They see the talent in young people or those wanting to better themselves and make time to help you or someone you adore. They also teach us how to become a mentor to others and make a powerful impact on someone's life.

Opposite sex co-worker – Such friendships can be complicated yet are rewarding because of their shared perspectives in meetings and decisions. The same can be true of a man who has female friends at work. There is nothing wrong with it and friendships at work can become great friendships outside of work. Obviously, there could be issues of attraction, misunderstanding, gossip, and jealousy. Therefore, any such work friendship must be clearly defined and understood by all involved. As a woman, my male friends provided a safe harbor when I was receiving unwanted attention from male leaders at work. Things to remember with this type of friendship: be aware of over familiarity, be mindful of appearances, and make good decisions. In my case, my marriage is strong, and I became friends with male co-workers who were also in strong marriages. In fact, I made sure we all met and became couple-friends. If you or your potential friend is single, or if one (both?) of you is in a troubled relationship, the risk may be too great. Remember to make good decisions.

Volunteer – These philanthropic giving individuals bring us into a world of giving and show us opportunities where we might help and make a difference. They pull us out of our bubbles and priorities to learn to serve in a fundraiser, community service, or fun event. These are usually very positive-minded givers that openly welcome you.

Financially astute – I love the friend who knows more about finances than I do. They want you to be financially wealthy, too, and from being around them, you learn to save more, invest wisely, and think about your money decisions.

Travel guru – This is another one of my favorites. If you can master the skills to become a Travel Guru or find a friend who is one now and make them part of your inner circle, you will easily travel to some very cool places in your lifetime. Stay open to collect the person who has joy in life and willingness to share what places they loved best and explain why. This interesting type of friend helps you see the world.

The Prayer Warrior – I love this term, Prayer Warrior. All of us have some superpowers. Some are amazing at baking the world's best lasagna, drawing a landscape within moments, talking to someone in distress, rescuing a dog, playing an instrument like a master, or simply bringing a smile to your face. There are also those amongst us that are skilled, favored, and can turn up the energy to offer the power of prayer. They seem to have a direct line to God when it comes to asking for a favor. They are what some call a "Prayer Warrior." There are sceptics, of course, but prayer never hurts, and I have seen some truly amazing things happen when Prayer Warriors take action.

Faith is a personal issue for most. Yet even people who don't grasp this belief will usually accept prayers when offered. I have never said, "I will pray for you," and had someone answer, "Please don't."

I remember my father lying in the emergency room, not looking well after having a stroke. The reverend stopped by, leaned over his gurney, and asked if he could help with a prayer. I'll never forget my dad's big brown eyes looking up to the ceiling. He slowly smiled and replied, "Ok, just a short one, Preacher."

We all laughed, and a quick, beautiful prayer was given. As if my dad was in some big rush and didn't have time for a longer prayer.

The cool part about having a Prayer Warrior in your friendship circle is that you have someone with almost superpowers to relate to your agony. They are always ready to offer a prayer of gratitude or a request for divine guidance.

So why else do we need to collect this type of person in our circle?

It's simple. The Prayer Warrior makes us a better person. They remind us to stop and praise the Almighty for the good things that have happened, and they sympathize when things are off in our life. They remind us we are not alone and are skilled at leading us to the specific holy words that can uplift or nourish our souls.

I remember when I caught the dreaded flu and could not speak. For an extrovert, this is a double whammy! Having to stay home in bed is bad enough, but not verbally communicating was super weird. I felt like a monk in my home; I could barely whisper, and my introvert husband started whispering back to me. I couldn't figure that one out, but then it dawned on me. Awe . . . that's what you do when someone whispers to you, you whisper back. It was awkward and funny at the same time.

With a high fever and still no voice, I knew I needed help in a more significant way, super-fast. So, this is what I did. I contemplated my collection of friends and sent texts, thus rallying my prayer warrior friends by asking for a healing favor. Multiple prayers were texted back to me, and I knew they were being said aloud for me daily. I whispered to them as best I could. My friends continued with follow-up texts over the week: "How are you doing now? Anything I can do to help? Need some hot soup dropped off? Need your dogs walked?"

TIP:

Remember, friends want to help you, especially true friends, but you need to ask. Friends are not mind readers.

So how do we locate this type of friend—the Prayer Warrior?
If you are a believer, express your faith to others in a loving, caring way when a moment seems appropriate. For example, if they say they are lucky, I like to say, "You mean blessed?"

They usually stop, consider my suggestions, rephrasing, and nod. I have never had anyone argue. That subtle expression of words signals your faith. If you both are of the same mindset and show gratitude, a friendship may begin. The light shines brightly amongst such people, and they are typically happy to stop what they are doing and give you a moment. That person may become your Prayer Warrior friend.

You can also pay closer attention to such signals when meeting healers, coaches, and physicians who believe in the power of prayer. Many of them are Prayer Warriors and when asked to offer a quick blessing on your behalf, they are happy to do so. I have found some physicians are Prayer Warriors and will gladly pray with me during a medical visit or treatment. I have experienced a surge of peace and expedited healing. Asking clinical workers to combine their talents with God's grace yields significant healing and strength. Many miracles have happened to those who have asked to receive. I worked in healthcare for decades, and the patients who miraculously recovered always mentioned they had an arsenal of people praying for their healing.

One of my Prayer Warriors has a designated spot to pray in their North Carolina home. She reserves time to be still, reflect, show gratitude, and pray for direction.

Healthy Versus Poor Fitting Couple Friends

Things that Make You Go Hmmm: Do you ever feel you have outgrown friendship with a couple? After spending time with them, do you feel drained? Maybe they bicker with each other or have grown apart over the years. As a result, hanging with them now feels strained.

Over the decades, we lost some of our couple-friends from uncontrollable forces like divorce, death, and relocation. At one point I said to my husband, "We need some healthy couple-friends who love each other." This was a specific vacancy in our inner circle. Letting go of close friends can break your heart or be liberating, depending on how healthy the friendship is. This can be even harder with couple-friends; one of them may be the problem but you lose both. Life sometimes calls for sacrifices.

Let me share two stories. The first one shows how unaware I was when things went sideways in a long-term friendship. The second shows how to do it the right way.

Poor Fitting Couple-Friends – "Out with the Old"

It was "the night of the ugly dinner party and card game." Obviously, my longtime friends had forgotten how to be good dinner guests because within hours of arriving their actions killed our friendship.

TIP:

Decline an invite early on if you are a couple constantly bickering or have not fully reconciled from a fight. If you have already accepted an invitation, either agree to set your differences aside for the evening or cancel. You are not doing your host or yourself a favor by showing up in a bad mood and ruining the event.

When I worked sixty hours a week, and our three girls were young, entertaining had to be a carefully orchestrated feat. I made the time a priority for our friends since they were a highly valued treasure in our lives. Since my life lacked enough hours to do all that was on the schedule, I had to plan things well in advance. This planning took tremendous energy and time to arrange a sitter, consider a menu, shop, cook, clean, and maybe even decorate our home. Time was more precious to me than money. I could always make more money. Yet, I could never get those precious hours back.

Things that Make You Go Hmmm: Take a moment, and dwell on those last lines. Many friends overlook the efforts and sacrifices made by the host having an event. Be mindful of them. This is something to remember and never take for granted as a true friend.

So, here's what happened that ended a friendship of twenty years. One horrible evening, we entertained a long-time couple we dearly adored, Marco and Maggie. Our couple-friends had been jabbing and bickering for the last few years, but this evening their behavior was simply outrageous. In fact, sadly, it became the death of our couple's friendships.

After serving an entirely home-cooked dinner, followed by coffee and dessert, we sat down to play cards. About thirty minutes into our game of Poker, Marco threw the empty box of cards at Maggie because she had shared an update that Marco was getting counseling. I was in the healthcare industry for twenty years and thought she was soliciting support for medical connections. Not a big deal, right? It made sense to me. BOY, oh BOY, was I wrong—this was a big deal. In fact, it was the last straw.

Hearing this, was sad news. One of us was struggling. That was appropriate for close friends to share such information. Yet in Marco's world of their rocky marriage, Maggie had violated something way too personal. Immediately, he voiced his outrage at my dinner table. Maggie reacted by throwing chips back at Marco. A verbal fight followed. They jumped up, gathered their belongings, and made haste out of our front door. Bam! You know the expression, "Don't let the door hit you!" I didn't have time to utter it.

We stood there in silence, stunned. A question popped into my head. "Why is this couple in our lives?" I looked at my husband, Donald. Like me, he was speechless. Then I realized something far worse had happened than just friends fighting. This couple, who once were our dear friends, had changed. They had become so unhappy that they now had no regard for our friendship or our efforts to host them. They ruined our Saturday evening plus took time out of our busy lives I could never get back. They were miserable and could not control their tornado-like impact on our world. Donald and I quietly worked for the next hour to clean up and silently realized where this led. They never called to apologize.

Granted, we all have bad weeks, months, sometimes years, and true friends stay with true friends through good times and bad, but sometimes friendships end. We will cover more of that in our Chapter 8 on a Death of a Friendship. Especially if they behave now in ways you cannot tolerate. Friends who drink too much, fight too much, act badly, mistreat others, and so on, sometimes have to be cut loose.

Months went by, and I privately met Maggie for a quick lunch to get a thermometer check. Everything seemed like she was my same dear friend until she blurted out, "I want a divorce." Then I saw the rage in her eyes. Maggie immediately minimized her vulnerable moment masking it with, "I don't know why I said that."

I knew. Likewise, I perceived she no longer felt safe to share her genuine emotions since we had been couple-friends, not girlfriends. I gave her the name and number of a female friend who is a divorce lawyer, someone I knew to be a good person. That was that. Because we had been friends for so long, I reached out a few times but never heard back. Not a surprise. Fifteen years of fabulous friendship all ended in a fit of rage. They were not mad at Donald and me. We were collateral damage. Our friendship was a casualty of their unhappiness.

Your time and energy are of great value. Choose who you spend them with wisely and value dear friends who choose to make you a priority. Too many times people stay couple-friends when that is no longer wise. It may be that the husbands are good friends, or the wives are good friends; any other combination is just asking for disaster. The spouses try to cooperate, but the four just cannot mix well. Forcing all to engage is not ideal, especially if any personal business is shared.

Recommendation? Let the individuals who enjoy each other's company have their time but don't mix as couples. Be honest with your spouse. Don't resent their friendship, but do not have an unwanted friendship forced upon you. That is assuming, of course, the friend doesn't possess terrible values. If that's the concern, you should not let your partner wander off to visit that friend without you by their side. If they are suitable and you don't enjoy mixing as a couple, give them permission and encouragement to see each other for lunch or a drink separately. This includes you calling to just invite them for girl's or guy's time. It's an odd thing, yet many times women stop being friends just because their men don't get along. That's a silly reason to not keep a fabulous friend in your life. You are entitled and encouraged to have your own friends outside of being couples.

When couple-friends split up, you can find yourself in a loyalty trap. A friend may demand that you choose between the two. "You can't be friends with me if you keep being friends with him." In this case, you have a very hard decision to make. Is one friend crushed by the breakup and needs your support? Do you consider one to be at fault and the other innocent? Both good? Both bad? You should have a very open discussion with your partner and decide how you are going to handle the situation. The last thing you want is for "their breakup" to harm your relationship with your spouse.

 PONDERING PAUSE:

NOT SURE IF YOU SHOULD JUST MEET SOLO? THERE IS A SIMPLE CALCULATION TO CONSIDER FOR YOURSELF AND YOUR PARTNER.

- How do I feel talking with only one of them?
- Would I welcome more alone time for deeper conversations?
- Did I notice I have to limit or censor our conversation topics when all four of us are present?
- Would I like to have a more candid discussion with just one of them? *Consider if you might enjoy having lunch one-on-one with your friend, not as couples. If yes, try it and see what happens.*

After the Maggie and Marco lesson, my husband and I decided it was time to make a conscious effort to seek new couples we'd both enjoy having as friends. We used the principles and processes covered in this book. We looked at identifying the values and qualities we most desired (reference Chapter 3) in new friends, along with our current inventory of friends (this Chapter 4). Doing that helped us decide and proclaim we wanted to meet positive-minded, loving couples that were wholesome, active, and kind. Even more specifically, we mentioned we liked couples with a sense of humor that liked to explore and travel. For us, it was time to add a new couple-friends into our inventory of friends.

How to Find Healthy Couple-Friends – "In with the New"
If you identify a couple that you think would be good friends, begin by sharing an invitation to a casual event. Something that will allow you to talk but also allows you, or them, to disengage if necessary. Consider an outdoor festival, an art gallery or museum, a fundraising event is a good choice. Something with plenty of room. Arrive separately. "This has been fun, but we have to go," needs to be an option. This is a great way to observe your potential friends. You can casually assess how well the spouses (or significant others) connect without the pressure of sitting at an arranged dinner. When you extend an invitation, you should plan on purchasing all tickets if they are required. Let them know they are your guest. Usually, they will reciprocate and insist on buying refreshments or invite you to another event of their choice.

If your casual events together have been successful and all of you would like to take your friendship to the next level, consider inviting your friends to join you on a short road trip. Here is an example of a successful outing:

 TIP:

A successful road trip requires planning but does not mean you should become a controlling planner. Think of your plan as a thoughtful guide and let your friends give input ahead of time. Plan the route, including stops on the way. Purchase tickets well ahead of time. Plan hotels and restaurants if possible and make reservations.

One of our most successful couple-friends road trips was to Richmond, Virginia, to see a traveling exhibit of the Terracotta Soldiers from China. It was the first time this exhibit had come to America, and we were eager to see it. We have a membership which allows us to attend the "members only pre-opening" of the exhibit. I was able to purchase four additional member tickets and invited two couples. Here's what made the day totally rock.

If you know your friends well, you will know who should do each job. One of our friends feels a great sense of accomplishment when she finds the best deals on hotels, restaurants, and side activities. Hunting through all the options and possibilities is like a computer game for her. Once we have a general outline, we turn her loose to chase down all the details. She never fails.

Another one of my best friends is Bruce, and he loves to be the driver on car trips. Since he is as tall as a bear, he doesn't easily fit in standard size vehicles, so he rents an SUV large enough to seat everyone in luxury. It's "his thing."

Having one large SUV we can all ride together, which makes a trip easier from not worrying about losing someone on the road. Following another car is no fun and stressful for drivers having continually to look behind to spot the following car fighting traffic to stay in sight of the lead car. God forbid they miss the exit. UGGH! You can spend forever finding each other again and not making your destination on time. To make everyone stay hydrated and energized, I always pack a cooler of drinks and snacks. Plus, if we all ride together no one misses sharing in the conversations.

 TIP:

Always offer to pay for gas or part of the rental. It's the right thing to do with your friends. You'd be surprised how many friendships erode because one friend always covers the cost, and another friend just tags along. On the other hand, if you know your friend cannot afford it, beat them to the point and state that you are covering the cost.

Did you catch the part about packing a cooler? My clever mom taught us that as children. We always carry cold drinks, fruit, cheese, crackers, and some chocolate in our road trip cooler.

Want to avoid people getting cranky? Don't let their blood sugar drop. If you are bringing a snack, bring enough to share. Everyone loves trying new things or at least wants to be asked if they would like something. It's a sign of friendship that you are inclusive in nature and have thought of others when packing.

Know when to take a break. I have traveled with people who act like camels. They fill up on food and drink before leaving and never want to stop until they reach the destination. If you are more of a camel, ask your companions when they would like to stop for food, fuel, or restrooms. Think of applying Maslow's Hierarchy of Needs and see how your friends like you even more.

 TIP:

Realizing others have bodily needs makes you a great host, too, and others will want to hang with you more.

Taking care of logistics makes everyone's trip better. It might sound basic, but you would be amazed how few people are good at planning. It's like a superhero skill, and you can be such a great friend trying to help plan. Nothing is as exhilarating as when a plan comes together. Vehicle, provisions, schedule, everyone in their seats, and off you go on a new adventure. It's awesome!

When mixing new friends, the less drama you have, the better for all concerned. Better planning means less drama and more fun. Make sure everyone knows the itinerary. Include names and phone numbers of people, events, restaurants, hotels and so on.

So back to the Richmond trip to see the Terracotta Soldiers. Our day together with the six of us was spectacular. The exhibit tickets had an entry time, and we arrived in Richmond well ahead of that. We spent the extra hours exploring historic sites, of which there are many in Richmond. We had a shared sense of exploration and even the introverts joined the conversations. Having an activity everyone can focus on opens up new friends' abilities to engage in conversations.

There was enough time to take in the Virginia War Memorial. The guys were more interested in military history than the ladies, but it was nice that they were having a good time too. They talked more and more, and time flew by. We made it to the exhibition on time, and it was everything we hoped it would be.

On the way home, we stopped at one of our favorite restaurants in Williamsburg, and by the time we got back home, our two sets of couple-friends had become couple-friends. We see each other often and have since shared many adventures.

Identifying the Holes to Fill in Your Inventory of Friends

My inner circle is known for welcoming newcomers when I introduce them at one of our group events. Over the years, they have grown to trust my judgement and assume the new person must be someone special. I fulfill this expectation by making sure the new friend possesses compatible qualities and values. We've discussed how helpful it is to identify current friends' qualities to make it more obvious about what is missing. That's why it is so important that you take time to finish writing out your qualities and traits list and declare the ones you value most. Using your personal list will allow you to identify ideal people for future friendships. It will save you time, money, and heartache. Likewise, your friends will begin to trust that who you introduce to them will be a good fit.

We've explored looking at your inventory of friends hopefully to widen your view of what else might be missing. You can also focus now to look for specific descriptors desired of potential friends (Artist, Golfer, Prayer Warrior, Travel Guru, Mentor, and other specifics). If you can welcome friendships that are unlike those in the past, your inner circle will be more interesting and help you grow personally. Collecting a mixture of friends with different backgrounds, countries of birth, experiences, and interests can also make you appear more interesting to others. Why? Because you will gain a more worldly perspective and have a greater knowledge base to carry on conversations.

We've laid a great foundation for knowing what our current friendships look and feel like. Now it's time to start exploring how we purposely move into the collecting true friendships mode. To do this, we must first be aware of another step to take on this new journey to collect true friends. It is the step of accepting that roadblocks and barriers can happen. In our next chapter, we will explore roadblocks that can pop up when we are attempting to meet someone or become a friend.

Fear Suspicion of Intent

Unawareness Reputation

Timing Manners & Customs Social Class

Roadblocks

Personality Styles

Education Level Proximity

Afraid of Giving Distrust

Afraid of Being Hurt

Let's explore what's holding you back from filling your inner circle.

You may encounter obstacles when attempting to pursue a new friendship. I call these "roadblocks." A roadblock can end a conversation you would like to continue. A roadblock can cause confusion and prevent friendships from forming. We've explored which qualities can keep people at a distance, and you've created a list of what qualities you want more of when collecting friends. Now let's talk about potential roadblocks you could encounter when getting to know someone, and what to do about it. Being trained to spot a barrier will save you time and frustration.

The first thing to learn is that it is not always your actions causing a roadblock. They can be emotionally driven or socially related. Therefore, do not take it personally if someone suddenly withdraws from getting any closer. Suppose you read the chapter on self-evaluation and passed with flying colors. In that case, you can safely assume the problem is them, not you, and your best course of action is to toughen your skin and understand that people can have invisible barriers that prevent them from forming a connection. Charging headlong into that barrier is not a good plan. On the other hand, if you encounter the same barrier over and over, maybe it is you. Keep this in mind and run through the self-evaluation again. Knowing about obstacles can help you in business situations, too. Business professionals, network with others using their hearts and minds as guides. Learning what emotional roadblocks restrict our ability to deepen a relationship, even at work, will make you a more accepting person.

Barriers, regardless of their cause, can last for a moment or forever. The good news is most barriers will soften over time as mutual trust develops. Think back to when we've talked about the four essentials necessary to cement a relationship into a friendship: know, like, trust, and be memorable. Again, you can see how important it is to advance a relationship into the trust phase, not let it stay at the acquaintance level.

 TIP:

You don't have to make friends with everyone you meet, yet if you see someone frequently, work on building mutual trust. It always comes in handy in the future.

Were you aware that our minds and hearts are actively engaged when meeting or talking with others? It sounds logical, yet we often forget how human we are and what guides our decisions about liking someone or something. Our past experiences are stored information for us to reference, much like a database. It provides vital information on how to proceed to know a person better. Much of this information is helpful for our safety and well-being. However, there can also be tainted information based on our inexperience or negative influencers we knew. Such information can negatively affect how we see others and limit us from having a meaningful relationship with someone who would be helpful in our world.

For example, at a school where I worked right out of college, I was hired by a determined leader named Natalie into a fast-paced office. She wanted me there, and I was eager to succeed. Unfortunately, from the first interview with her Assistant Director Ricki, it was apparent he disliked me. Why did he hate me so much? I was too young and naïve to understand office politics. Had I taken a moment and thought back to remembering being the *Little Viking Girl,* I might have realized his facial reaction looked the same as those I'd met as a child. They disliked me not for who I was but for how I looked.

Finally, one day Ricki blew up in front of the entire office, threw some papers towards me, and said, "You are just like my ex-wife, that hateful redheaded Bitch!" Wow! You could have heard a pin drop on the carpet. His hatred for me was proclaimed and explained, showing the roadblock that would forever prevent him from connecting well with me. He was biased based on what his mind and heart fed him from earlier experiences. When he saw me, he saw his ex-wife, and felt pain.

Many times in life, you may NEVER discover the reason behind someone's actions. All we can do is what God mandates. It's best to practice the golden rule "do unto others as you shall have them do unto you," even when someone acts like a jerk. When you find yourself truly lost why others do what they do, give them grace and some space. That approach allows you to accept them where they are living while also giving you a safe distance if they are emotionally driven. Remember, others are watching how you behave and deciding if they want to know you better. After that exciting day in the office, I noticed my coworkers were overall kinder to me, and we bonded more. I attribute that to my prior actions with Ricki. I did not encourage Ricki's negative attitude by giving him fuel or mentioning his rude antics to others. They saw it for themselves.

Barriers hinder how we react or get perceived by others. Sometimes roadblocks can act as a safety net to prevent those people from ever moving near, which can be a good thing!

Over the past decades, I have become wiser and realized our heavenly father sets his angels around us like a hedge of protection to repel certain people from coming nearer. Have you ever met someone you liked socially or in a business setting and set up a date to get together? Then it never happens, for a valid reason. You reschedule, and it gets canceled again and again. After the third or fourth time, it feels harder to want to meet. Then finally, you both forget to reschedule. Life got in the way. Or so you thought. Not until much later do you see them, and you both comment that your schedules or timing never worked, yet you don't feel compelled to reschedule. That's what many call "God's wink."

Learn to question "why" repeated roadblocks are placed in front of you that prevents you from connecting deeper. Perhaps the timing was off, or that person was not supposed to move nearer to your world. Pay attention and observe them closely. Several times, a valid reason became apparent as to why I should never engage with that person. I was saved from the mistake of knowing them. Wow! Even though at the time it was confusing, later I felt blessed for divine roadblocks. Have you ever had a situation where you kept trying to meet up with someone, and it did not work out? Consider that may have been exactly as it was supposed to be in your best interest.

Remember, our goal is to develop awareness and discernment when connecting and looking for friends with specific qualities. What happens next is the need to weave in, becoming mindful of potential roadblocks or barriers. I recommend you frequently practice those skills with anyone you meet or talk with. First, use awareness, then discern their words and actions, and watch for any obstacles popping. Hopefully, you won't see or feel many barriers since most people openly welcome a friendly, short conversation. You can practice building your skills with a repairman, the mail person, grocery clerk, doctor's staff, coworkers, or a person in the waiting room. Practicing your skills with strangers allows you to be more relaxed to engage with someone you view as a potential friend.

Here are some of the top barriers, or roadblocks shared over the past twenty years. The list of obstacles can be broader. Think of those listed as common denominator barriers which prevent you from drawing quality people closer into your life, like a magnet. During a conversation, a barrier (temporary or lasting) could result from:

- Suspicion of intent.
- Distrust (until comfortable).
- Confusion over manners and customs.
- Insecurity due to being some place new with a new person.
- Concern for one's reputation (theirs or yours).
- Concern over social status differences.
- Concern over educational differences.
- Concern over personality styles not mixing.
- Lack of confidence.
- Introvert versus extrovert differences.
- Sense of intimidation (feeling dominated).
- Fear of rejection by others.
- Saying too much / Fear of saying too much.
- Fear of being hurt or being used.
- Fear to give or being asked to give.
- Fear they have little value (doubt of worth).
- Fear of not fitting in with others.
- Social obstacles:
  - Lack of proximity to see each other.
    - Lack of access.
    - Lack of fitting in.

- Lack of willingness to engage.
- Lack of reciprocation:
  - Poor follow-up skills.
  - Poor timing now.
  - Little open time.
  - Inadequate funds.

So, who first puts up the roadblock? Sometimes the other person puts up the barrier. Sometimes we are the ones unconsciously blocking another, much like a force field around the body. I firmly believe everyone has experienced a mind or heart roadblock when connecting with others. We just don't always recognize it while it is happening. Usually, awareness does not occur until later, when we try to process and reflect. For example, many authors experienced doubt (fear of being unworthy) many times while writing their books. I know I certainly have.

Many other authors were well-established in relationships building and established as public figures. Some days I felt euphoric becoming an author knowing the value of sharing this unique perspective on *Collecting True Friends* into the world. Other days I felt inadequate compared to those who came before me. Those are roadblocks I created. When I had the fortunate opportunity to meet a famous author in a social media forum, I knew God arranged this. I wanted to join the author's discussions since I admired her for so long. Yet, I was hesitant and unsure how an industry influencer would receive me. Even though I was determined to become part of this famous author's room discussion, my stomach rolled when thinking about connecting. My awe of the author's achievements in our industry blocked my ability to welcome this blessing, this opportunity to meet each other. My self-imposed barrier could have crippled my pathway to connect. Most surprising is that even super confident people (like me) have to push themselves out of their comfort zones and push through a roadblock. My wise husband noticed my doubt then pointed out the author's background probably varied from mine, and she might welcome my fresh perspective. I followed this fantastic author on social media, and we finally met and talked. I joyfully discovered she welcomed my input and friendship. She is an excellent, generous, kind person like I imagined. Why would I allow such ill-serving emotions or thoughts to strangle my desire to connect broader into the world? That's the question we all need to ask ourselves when a barrier bubbles up (self-imposed) or is released (by another). The next time you feel a roadblock bubbling up inside you, ask yourself if a positive outcome gained would be worth your temporary discomfort.

PONDERING PAUSE:

- Can I now see how an obstacle blocks making excellent connections and friends? __Yes __No ____ Somewhat
- When has this happened to me in the last few years?
- I remember when I listened to ill-serving thoughts (or felt heart pangs), and it almost kept me from meeting (insert their name).
- Did I realize at first it was a roadblock? ____Yes ____No____ Somewhat
- The roadblock (see list above) I felt happening was
  _____.
- The roadblock was telling me to not get near this person, because I was concerned about _____.

The Surprise Feeling When a Roadblock Hits

What does it feel like when someone has roadblocked your attention? Were you caught by surprise? Explore this scenario with me. You enjoy talking and believe you are in a great conversation with an acquaintance. Then the energy between you both changes to an awkwardness. It confuses you because you cannot grasp what caused their surprising withdrawal. You question in your mind if you said something wrong or are they now bored talking with you? You've just experienced the feeling of a roadblock.

The first thing to do when a roadblock pops up is double-check yourself. Reflect to make sure your behavior didn't provoke the person to a roadblock. Consider your body language or words chosen. If you feel the roadblock wasn't generated from your actions, this is how I suggest you proceed. If still near one another, I find it ideal to lean in to gently ask the person, "Have I said something incorrect or inappropriate?" It allows them the ability and moment to be truthful if you've blundered. Don't keep talking. Just await their reply. That allows a moment for them to internalize what just happened and whether they are willing to share a clue to their weird behavior. When I used this questioning technique, I received two insightful answers.

One woman said with a still furrowed brow, "Not at all. I was just trying to process what you had said. I've never thought about it that way. What a fresh perspective." She then smiled, and we continued talking.

Another time, a businessman and I were talking at an event, and when I spoke of the work his company was known for, he visibly withdrew. I confused another organization's mission and milestones with this similarly named company hosting this event. The businessman confirmed I had indeed made a blunder. He politely said, "Yes, that is incorrect and is not our mission here. I can share with you what I learned being on their Board if that might be of help. Are you interested in learning more?"

Boy, was I! I didn't want to repeat any wrong information again. I felt appreciation for this man. It was such a diplomatic way he handled, letting me know how uninformed I was.

I was eternally thankful that I had been brave enough to ask a clarifying question, "Did I say something inappropriate?" Notice how gracious he was to offer to help update my knowledge about their organization. An excellent lesson to commit to memory and practice frequently is to allow someone grace when they say something wrong. If they say something that makes you pop up a roadblock, first approach them with grace. It will make you memorable in a great way. Being gracious is an outward Godly sign to others like a huge beacon that beams you are "worthy of knowing."

Let me help you see how another behavior created a roadblock for my friend trying so hard to make friends. In this situation, the same barrier kept happening when she joined conversations and remained clueless. She would jump from one unrelated topic to another. Listening to her felt almost overwhelming as I tried to follow her thoughts. She'd speak to the point of exhaustion and not pause for a moment to hear anyone's viewpoint or even breathe, seemingly.

Seeing this happen repeatedly, I became curious as to what causes this behavior. After I felt we trusted one another, I finally asked Joyce if she knew how constant talking could block others. I gently shared that it might be holding her from allowing acquaintances to get closer and gaining more friends. Her answer stunned me. People may have misjudged Joyce's rambling, thinking she was self-centered. Instead, it was not at all what I imagined was a trigger. Joyce's non-stop talking was triggered when she felt unnerved, usually happening around influential people. Interesting! That was similar to my experience when I hesitated to meet the revered author I wished to befriend. Except I acted opposite to my nature. I am an extrovert who behaved like I didn't feel comfortable engaging. Joyce wanted to listen more but admitted she could not control her mouth due to nerves. The more she talked, the faster her words came.

I proposed a solution. Joyce and I agreed to help each other be more aware. I offered we could share a secret word (a signal) I'd say to clue her in when her endless talking happened. That signal helped clue her to become aware. She learned to control her nervous talking, thereby creating fewer roadblocks when interacting with others. Seeing how others responded favorably gave her the confidence to know people did like her, and she made more friends. She just had to become more approachable and not cause people to put up barriers.

It was eye-opening to learn more about what causes people to ramble. Regardless of what we've been told, it does not always mean talkers are self-absorbed. Realizing that babbling can be a symptom of anxiety and nervousness caused by meeting someone they admire has reminded me to be gentler and listen more. Powerfully confident people can show up with too much energy and make a stranger nervous. Many times, my bold confidence intimidated someone I was fascinated with and wanted to know better. That was never my intent. I am more aware now and make it a habit to pull back my large presence when I feel it might intimidate.

 TIP:

I recommend looking inwards at the dominant traits that might create an obstacle to others getting to know you. If you are unsure of what to modify, ask people around you what you are known for when talking and meeting others. If it is something that creates a barrier, become mindful. Then set a goal to correct it consciously. It is a great time to let go of ill-serving emotions and barriers that stop you from meeting incredible people. You are here to learn the art of collecting true friends who could be worthy of your time and devotion.

 PONDERING PAUSE:

- What trait do others say I always display (when talking with others) and that I want to fix or become better at?

  _____

- Can I find a trusted friend or family member to share this improvement goal with and ask them for help? ____Yes ____No.

- My secret word (or signal) when I do that ill-serving behavior will be _____.
- By this date _____, I want to feel like I have improved on being better at _____.

Recognizing the difference between introverts and extroverts and their polar approaches to meeting new people will help avoid hitting a barrier with someone. Pay attention to their energy level. Are they enjoying time talking just with you (introvert) or looking to include more people (extrovert) in the conversation circle?

Here is one of my favorite truth bombs about the difference in their styles. When an introvert says something, they mean it. Why? Because they have thought it out in their heads and might have even talked it aloud to themselves. However, when an extrovert talks, that is how they feel and think at that moment and until they finish "cooking" their thoughts, it is temporary. Do not take an extrovert's first comment as to their final decision. Give them time to think it through and ask them for their decision. It will avoid many barriers and unnecessary roadblocks caused by confusion because they think and process completely differently.

 TIP:

Here are some proven tips to make you more of a magnet to your opposite style. Realize that when introverts speak, they have waited their turn and now want to be heard and listened to. The introvert feels they say so little, usually that when they do speak, they WANT to feel confident others will listen. When an introvert is heard, that makes them want to connect further.

If you are an extrovert, pay attention to how others respond, especially introverts. You might need to dial back your energy to relate easier and not overwhelm them. Likewise, if you are an introvert and want the extrovert to stay engaged longer, aim to dial up your energy level when they speak. Lean-in more, nod your head, slowly smile, or tilt your head, are all clear signs you are interested. This sounds logical enough, yet each style frequently wants the other style to be the one that adjusts. Consequently, neither connects during a roadblocked friendship opportunity.

Acknowledging we can be the creators of obstacles will change how we connect with others. Likewise, having the patience to give grace to those who may be creating roadblocks without knowing it can positively affect our magnetism. Even people with high self-esteem can wonder, "Have I done something wrong?" when they are left hanging for an answer. A no-response behavior can happen in business networking as well as social mingling. For example, a professional prepares for an upcoming meeting as they agreed, and her contact fails to call back or take her call. A potential customer disappears not because they aren't interested but perhaps that previously hot deadline project is no longer a company priority. However, the potential customer forgot to communicate with others affected. In business, that forgetfulness is considered poor manners and damages reputations or injures goodwill. Socially, that same conduct can play havoc with a person's mind. In the absence of information, we tend to fill in the gaps. Usually, we get it wrong.

I had the pleasure to moderate a club in a social media app called Clubhouse filled with thirty women of various ages. I punted up the concept of "What bubbles up when a person is slow to, or forgets to, reply back?" Neither age nor experience varied their responses that our first instinct is to internalize a reason why we hear "crickets." We feel a sense of rejection. That is so curious in human nature. Very confident people believe that a no reply or slow reply equals less interest. Why so? Deep down, our human desire is to be liked by others. When another person fails to respond, we usually think it was intentional. Most of my panelists replied they considered a no-reply as the other person didn't want to hear from them, or something had changed in their relationship.

Another common belief was that people failed to respond because they felt the other wasn't enough of a priority. How sad if that last belief was true, right? The consensus also showed few people would follow up again unless a relationship was in the trust phase.

So, if you are interested in someone or something, following up is the big lesson here. Interesting, right? Rejection plays such a significant role as an obstacle for others getting to know and then like you. Likewise, confusion over someone being interested in being their friend is another barrier to consider, like Tina's story below.

Tina is an established, successful business owner, well-respected in our community and liked by all. She draws a crowd wherever she goes because of her huge smile and high energy. Today people think Tina collected friends quickly throughout her whole life; however, she was not always this approachable and inclusive.

There was a time in her twenties that she hung out only with her clique of friends. They were beauties who played on the beach, acted self-centered, and enjoyed life to its fullest. That time in her life felt more like a continuance of high school days even though they all graduated and were employed. It felt like great fun, yet her lifestyle missed something. She had a limited understanding of the necessity and value of welcoming girl-friendships. Back then, Tina's self-centered world was filled with the same types of friends inside her exclusive ring. "People who say they don't like cliques are the ones who can't be in a clique," was their motto. Whoa! That unwelcoming attitude adopted during their teen days fostered an unhealthy mindset. Tina had a false abundance of friendships. There was quantity but not quality in her friendships. Tina believed having an inner circle meant she had enough friends. That was not a good belief to hold onto because it limited her ability to make better friends. Tina's group of similar friends were always available to spend time with, and they thought alike. She was socially comfortable and stopped inviting others to be closer to her world. Sadly, what was missing is what we've explored in Chapters 2 and 3. Tina ignored the necessity to identify and collect true friends. She could not determine what qualities were essential in her friends and overlooked inviting variety into her world.

One day, Susie asked Tina to go to the movies. Tina ignored the request because she did not understand it. Tina thought that was something you do on a date. You don't go to the movies with a girlfriend. Tina didn't understand why Susie wanted to be her friend and had yet to understand the value of spending time with any friend separately. Instead, her group of friends always showed up at a designated place and time in a lively cluster. She was suspicious and reserved an answer to Susie's invite because of inward confusion. Tina started to roll questions around in her head and heart. She sought answers. *"Do girlfriends do things together, like go to a movie or grab dinner? No one I know has girlfriends like that!"* It made no sense to her, even though she had known and trusted Susie for a while.

Tina couldn't figure out the answers alone, so she finally asked Susie why she wanted to be her friend. Susie smiled and pointed out what they had in common, and how Tina made her laugh. That surprised Tina. She sadly hadn't paid that much attention to Susie. In contrast, Susie had been more observant and felt compelled to "collect" Tina as a friend.

 PONDERING PAUSE:

- Has anyone you met in a group of people tried to reach out to invite you to something?
- Did you find it as a surprise they found you interesting outside of that group?
- Fill in the blanks:
- I reacted to their invitation with these emotions _____, _____, _____.

The roadblocks experienced in Tina/Susie's story show the roadblock created by a bubble of confusion followed by a lack of trust. Since Tina never individually developed deeper relationships within (or outside) her similar type community of friends, trust remained superficial. She felt comfortable mixing in the group yet, awkward seeing a friend in a one-on-one activity.

 **NOTE:**

Fortunately for Tina, Susie was tenacious and followed through inviting her again. We talked earlier about how a no-response can be perceived as a rejection or rudeness. This story is a great example of the slow-to-reply was not rudeness by Tina. Tina delayed because she felt confused. She delayed responding because she had no idea how to act or collect a true friend.

Remember when we covered the four essentials that must happen before any connection moves forward organically? They are: know, like, trust, and be memorable. That's precisely what this story shows. The third essential, trust, had not been rooted enough in those women's relationships. They knew each other well and liked each other being part of a large group. However, the trust component hadn't gelled. Susie was ready to move forward to the trust level while Tina remained confused, putting up a mental roadblock.

Mindsets can act as significant barriers that prevent friendships from forming. We often don't even realize when it happens until someone finally asks us, "Hey, what's going on?"

We might delay our answer because we are preoccupied with a daunting schedule or a bad experience and blocking our vision of an ideal connection.

Another thing that confounds me is when people think they have enough friends for now and avoid being open-minded to allow others to become closer. In Tina's case, she thought having a group of friends replaced the need for finding true friends with qualities she desired.

Eventually, Tina trusted Susie enough to accept her invitation to hang out together. Tina was surprised by how comforting it was to share genuine quiet conversations. The real engagement was a rarity in her friendships. She started walking, shopping, regularly calling, and sharing their dreams. They both quickly realized they could listen more when not distracted by the group's interruptions. Over time, their questions pushed each to feel safe enough to take risks towards personal growth. Active listening expedited their bond. The great news is Tina and Susie took a chance and made time to become friends outside of a large clique. Years passed, their party clique faded away, and yet their friendship remains to this day. These faithful friends have helped each other through major life challenges and joys. Tina's initial mindset, "Why do you want to be my friend? What do you want from me?" almost cost her one of her most treasured lifetime friends.

Don't Feel Rejected When They Are Suspicious.
It is easy to take something personally when someone you've met does not warm up to you as quickly as you would have liked. If you are destined to become friends, God will make a perfect time happen and push your paths to cross. Be patient.

I encountered a similar experience to Susie's pursuit with a colleague of mine, Kimberly. I asked Kimberly, an acquaintance, to go to coffee or lunch, and she reacted like that was a bizarre request. She pursed her lips, tilted her head, took a deep breath, and said nothing. She just stared at me. Her behavior could have repelled anyone. Most of us would have interpreted her outward appearance as a rejection. It is easy to interpret someone's resistance as a personal rejection of your offer. Luckily having my background of being bullied as the *Little Viking Girl*, I realized how people act initially is not always how they behave later. Sometimes you just need to give them space, and the more they see you, the more they feel comfortable.

It's Not Usually Rejection
Being in sales taught me not to see or hear a "No." Instead, what I choose to hear is "Not now."

 TIP:

I recommend you adopt the belief that it could be a poor timing issue if someone is slow to respond. Try your best not to take indifference personally. Over the next two years, I'd see Kimberly occasionally at other events, and we'd exchange pleasant greetings. I'd smile and let her know she could text me if she would like to catch up more. Letting her know the door was open is a technique that has worked well for me and others who adopted this approach.

The Grace and Space Approach
Everyone has their own busy life and obligations. It may not be an ideal time for them to make a new friend. If you've tried to initiate something with someone you've met, consider perhaps they did not respond because they are crazy busy with deadlines. Or are dealing with a family event that consumes all free time. Or maybe they are like Tina and haven't been observant enough to notice you are an ideal person worthy of getting to know. You may have caught them by surprise, as I did with Kimberly. We all must have enough personal bandwidth (time) to follow up with meeting new friends. Perhaps they are afraid they would have little time to be your good friend at that moment. No one wants to start a friendship and leave the other person hearing crickets.

TIP:

I highly suggest you adopt the "grace and space" approach when an unknown barrier exists. If someone does not accept your invitations or niceties the first few times, it may have nothing to do with you. Give them some grace and space. You can always say, "We should have lunch sometime," without trying to set an actual date. That shows desire without a demand. Think of it as "positive neutral."

When Kimberly saw me again in a meeting, she said, "I was thinking about us going to lunch; that's something friends do, and I don't know you as a friend. We've always worked together. Why do you think we should go to lunch?"

Since we'd known each other for years, I was stunned by her suspicious tone and directness in her question. Yet, I chose to ignore her abruptness and cautious attitude because I knew the value I bring to a friendship.

 **NOTE:**

Most people would have stopped there in wanting a friendship because they would feel rejected. Instead of letting rejection dominate my emotions, I told her I thought she had a great sense of humor and liked her interesting stories. Whenever she'd like to grab lunch, she could call.

My heart sensed Kimberly might lack quality friends. I also suspected something in her past made her fearful of welcoming new friends. Or perhaps she'd been taken advantage of by someone she let into her inner circle. Clearly, she kept building roadblocks when connecting with others. Either way, I wanted nothing from Kimberly and wanted the best for her. Here's a truth bomb. Over time your intentions become more evident than words. An expressed interest and steadfast positivity will usually compel others to see you again. Time and consistency reveal what's inside a person's heart to those who carefully watch. Giving someone space and grace to come to you when they are ready shows you honor them as they work through their roadblock.

Not Everyone Can Let Go of a Roadblock

You can't encourage everyone to reciprocate your kindness or invitations. However, when you stay aligned on your own life course with a pure heart, divineness becomes your guide leading you to the next person you must know better. Our heavenly Father doesn't have to learn awareness and discernment like we on Earth. He already has the plan lined up and knows which people we should meet and keep in our life. It's our job to make it easier for Him to place us in the right spots, so that magic happens. That is why we must know (and list) what qualities and values we hold dearly and likewise demonstrate those in our daily actions. I know this might sound flowery but remember this fact. Like attracts like. When you have the positive stuff inside you and proclaim you are ready to *Collect Your True Friends*, you will be a lighthouse to all the right ships at sea. That is what I call "becoming a magnet to others worthy of your time and devotion." To do so, we must first be worthy as well.

We are required to accept the times when we don't understand what's going on in our world. You may be compelled to meet another like I was to befriend Kimberly, even though it has nothing to do with your own benefit. Instead, it has everything to do with the other person's benefit. You are supposed to get to know them better to help them, not like a fixer or a rescuer, but as a messenger. Think of it like you are a secretly hired carrier to give a timely message. You become a vehicle sent to share a needed message. Unknowingly delivering a message of hope, an answer sought, or a missing piece in their journey of faith. When she removed her roadblock, Kimberly and I eventually became friends. When she trusted me enough to open up authentically, I realized how much she needed a solid, wholesome friend.

After hearing me talk about my treasured friends, Kimberly then asked if I'd introduce her to them. I agreed, asking if she could adopt healthier qualities. My goal was for her to be well-received when meeting my friends, so I asked if she was open to updating her friendship qualities. Notice I used the word updating, not improving. When we help a friend become a better version of themselves, I found that using the word update is gentler than improving. No one wants to admit we must improve. It implies we haven't done it correctly in the past, and that kills our self-esteem. If we ask someone to update their skills, that approach sounds hopeful, encouraging, and doable. So, remember, choose words that open doors and do not create more mental roadblocks.

Collecting True Friends is definitely a journey and an intentional mindset as you've been learning. So far, you've developed a foundation of what qualities and traits you want to see more of, what types of friendships you'd welcome, and spotting potential roadblocks along the way. Now let's move onto how to be the "real deal," whether meeting someone in person or virtually.

CHAPTER 6
AUTHENTIC FRIENDSHIPS IN A VIRTUAL WORLD

Social Media Can Cause Barriers and Confusion About Who is Your Friend

Social media has created an alternate reality for us, where we have thousands of friends but can still feel lonesome. How many of those virtual "friends" would take our phone call if we were in dire need? Facebook should really call it a "connect" button instead of a "friend" button. Since social media coins everyone as a friend or a follower, it confuses what norms are acceptable to build and keep a friendship. Plus, you have a wide range of different types of people that seek "friendship." The variety of people obscures our seeing motives since theirs are not always the same as ours. How so? We can present ourselves in any manner online as we design. Some show up with a perfect façade of family, home, career, life, etc. Others choose to be highly open to the point we want to shout "TMI (too much info)." Some people use online media strictly as a business necessity and some strictly engaging in socialization.

Consequently, everyone shows up online for various reasons sharing various levels of information. Ultimately, we choose and create either an actual or altered reality for the world to see. That's why some have playfully called one platform "Fakebook." Truth Bomb: the more you connect with a certain type, the more you will be connected. For example, I befriended some healers helping others with depression, and the technology algorithms thought I wanted to be connected to everyone suffering from trauma or grief. Instead, I was just supporting some colleagues with their businesses. Once I stopped following and responding to such postings and commented on things of interest, I was shown people and posts I enjoyed.

Collecting Friends Within a Virtual World

Let's explore how to apply our *Collecting True Friends* mindset in a virtual world. It's vital that what you choose to present online virtually allows your qualities to shine. This is very important for believers. It is possible to be proud of your faith while aiming to be gracious and tolerant online. Others aligned will feel compelled to know you better. To those new to being online, connecting virtually with others can confuse your psyche because you cannot hear an instant verbal response making it always hard to understand meanings. We "chat" or "message," yet it's not a live conversation, and unlike in a written letter, our words can be edited when posting online. This is an important point I want to make. When someone sends you a message or does a post, it can be carefully crafted for delivery. That is very unlike real life. Real conversations are fluid and not scripted. We will talk more about this in detail later.

Social media measures our success by making friends by the number of virtual connections and followers to confuse our mindsets further. Social media clearly promotes a quantity over quality kind of mentality. The more "friends" you get, and the more "likes" and "loves" you receive on what you post, the greater your popularity. Sometimes it feels like being back in high school with how everyone compares themselves to others based on their "success" in shallow relationships. All those likes, posts, and comments feed into algorithms that measure someone's ability to create virtual engagement with friends. That logic makes sense in a social media world; however, it would look bizarre if friendship was approached like that in person. It would be the equivalent of deciding to gain more friends and popularity by heading out to a shopping mall. While there, you round up as many people as possible, put them into a room, call them your friends, and ask them to applaud you in the food court. That would be truly weird unless you were paying them and telling them they were participating in a show. The act of gathering people into our lives does not make them our friends. That's why our psyche and emotions can be confused when interacting on social media.

Since social media actively markets the merest connection as "friends," we can struggle with our ultimate goal of building genuine relationships. If your goal is to deepen an existing relationship, frequent posts can absolutely be a beautiful way to stay on their radar. Consistency and frequency of communications allow the trust to grow and increase your ability to build friendships online. Tender and heartfelt follow-ups with others online can create a bond that can lead to a true friendship. What is a waste of our energies is the act of "posting and ghosting." It is a waste of time and confusing to others attempting to get to know you better because it ties back to the concept of hearing "crickets" from a no-reply.

Being virtual can be a beautiful way to nurture a relationship. Starting a friendship from scratch, however, is much more difficult. Unless you have mutual connections or a common interest in pulling you together, the other person may not participate. So, the best way to make a new friend online is to share your common denominator when initially connecting. For example, you are part of a private social media group or group study, and someone shares an interest in rescue dogs. You've adopted several rescue dogs, so their posts resonate with how you think and feel. That's a common denominator and an entry to begin a friendship online. When you have not been introduced to someone, look for potential areas that make you mutually attractive. Get ready to highlight or take some notes on these ideas and tips on attracting others to connect, plus what doesn't fit so well in a virtual world.

Benefits of Gaining Friendships in a Virtual Platform
Virtual connections:
- Has no geographical limits restricting who you can meet.
- Opens the world to friends in other countries and more accents, cultures, and ways to think.
- Prevents you from collecting the same types of people and reduces groupthink.

- Brings a higher volume to assess if they are your tribe with desired qualities.
- Allows you to keep friends after a career or family relocation.
- Saves you time quickly to check-in as a thoughtful friend.
- Helps you find a lost contact. For example, I virtually found and connected with three treasures from my past: my childhood bestie Diane in Maine, my half-brother Gene in Florida, and half-sister Theresa in Kentucky.
- Opens a window to glimpse how a person handles stress, crisis, or worldly affairs.
- Allows for easier cross-pollination of your inner circle of friends.
- Allows you to identify who your friends mutually know.
- Allows you to help more people by hosting a group to share a common interest, event, or cause.
- It is easier to be a thoughtful friend because you don't even have to remember special dates. Social media is fabulous for alerting you with daily reminders on friends' birthdays or work anniversaries.
- Instead of solely responding like everyone else on social media platforms, record a message or video and text or DM (direct message) it to that person. It will mean so much more than a written post. I love standing by something lovely, hitting the microphone button (in my text) and recording my good wishes with music playing. Everyone loves that extra touch, and it only takes five minutes. Many friends save my audio message to play for their families. That is an example of how you can easily make yourself memorable in a great way when collecting true friends.

 TIP:

Pay particular attention to your gut reaction when you repeatedly read or hear something virtually. If a comment makes your face wince because it feels polar to your beliefs, pause to consider not allowing that friendship or group connection to percolate further. For example, if I see someone posting something that looks too dark, close to witchery, or evil sounding, I immediately disconnect. If you've made a poor choice connecting online in the past, don't fret. We all get fooled. When it happens, it makes us wiser about what to look out for next time. *Collecting True Friends* takes practice, and just like in a sport, you have plenty of strikeouts before you learn to hit in that sweet spot on the bat. When virtually connecting, remember to practice using your three tools daily: awareness, discernment, and keen observation.

Lessons Learned on Friendships During the Pandemic

We learned a lot about how friends react differently during a time of mandated social distancing. I asked hundreds of people how they were feeling during those long months of 2020–21. Many people shared a surprising truth. The revelation shared was they learned who their true friends were and were not, based on who reached out. We all handle suffering differently. During the pandemic, some were reserved and checked in on their inner circles for giving and receiving support. Many sought comfort entirely online and openly shared emotional challenges via social media. Those who chose to stay in their "own bubble" did not connect with anyone and later realized they disappointed their friends and colleagues by disappearing. Consequently, some became forgotten friendships.

I also witnessed situations when friends were not empathetic enough to a potential friend attempting to engage. They were either not interested in making new friends or unaware of how much the other person was suffering and needed a friend. They missed the social clue that someone was reaching out to be their friend. The people who embraced someone being bold enough to start a conversation (virtually or on the phone) made some genuine friendships during the pandemic. Or perhaps self-imposed roadblocks prevented them from realizing someone was reaching out to them.

Stress brings people together. Friendships can be expedited by a common event with struggles, like the COVID disaster. Being authentic while staying positive during "those unprecedented times" increased the trust factor to make and keep friends. Being vulnerable and expressing how we handled things was welcomed by those needing direction on how to cope. Having the technology to connect virtually was also a blessing making it possible to connect easily.

Here are some key points learned during the pandemic and worth remembering:

- *Authentically* connecting is even more vital for being memorable and seen as a true friend.
- Reaching out to engage in others' critical moments (sad or happy) prevents us from becoming forgotten.
- Being more aware of someone asking to be your friend. It could be a great opportunity to connect genuinely. Plus, it increases your chance for a friendship to be reciprocated later.

Everything is Not Always What It Seems – Be the Real You
In 2015, I was blessed to resign from the stressful corporate world and became an independent consultant, creating the Red Hawk Strategic Solutions Company. Being online was a powerfully helpful tool I used to expand my exposure to meet new people. I immediately launched images and messages, re-inventing myself as a business owner. Social media was the ideal platform for messaging and connecting with strangers about my new venture. Who I was becoming and my value as a growth consultant, would be my message. No longer was I the corporate exec, but now a business growth consultant, speaker, and trainer. I updated my former colleagues and friends with my online posts showing what I was busy building. They saw the excitement and glamorous side of starting a business with images of me speaking or attending events. To new connections, the image they saw online was the person they would eventually meet in person.

Meanwhile, Behind the Scenes

What they saw online, however, was not the same as how I felt. I was scared to pieces of being self-employed. Even though my world felt like a roller coaster, I was determined to appear composed and enthusiastic to my online friends and followers. With divine direction and my true friends' support and love, I built a new identity with social media playing a significant role in rebranding. Being online and making new friends and connections felt daunting because I had to learn many new social media platforms. The mental roadblocks of not knowing what or when to post and which buttons to hit intimidated me, from being confused over what to post and when I would start and stop posting.

Why do you think I chose to minimize posting about my business and emotional struggles? It was because new people meeting me (online or in-person) would assess who I was without understanding my background or capabilities. Whereas those who were already my friends intuitively knew my tenacity would drive me to succeed. So, until I was a successful business owner, I felt I needed to control what others saw. I was not fully transparent about pitfalls and challenges. I showed what I wanted the world to see while I learned new skills. During the past years, social media has encouraged everyone to embrace a greater acceptance of showing our struggles, doubts, and challenges. Seeing someone's human side of their journey is welcomed.

My point is when you are virtually connecting, remember that those you meet online only show you what they want you to see. For example, if you'd been connected in person with me, you would have gathered a complete version of who I was. Both were accurate versions of me but were somewhat incomplete without video or in-person interaction. When you develop friendships in a virtual world, remember you may not have had an opportunity to get the complete picture. Let a relationship grow first before you overwhelm strangers with your entire life loaded with struggles, current challenges, and triumphs. From my experience, it is best not to post too much good, bad, and ugly information all at once. Use a balanced approach in what is shared so others can observe you and decide whether they like and trust you enough to know you better.

Some Surprising Lessons to Remember Virtually Connecting with Potential Friends, Family, Colleagues, and Partners:

- Social media recommends who to connect with based on the contacts loaded into your phone. It's a little creepy how well artificial intelligence (AI) determines who to recommend. Also, mutual connections will trigger more recommendations. So, make sure you know someone before connecting, or they will be recommended to your close connections too.
- Ask someone which social media they frequent the most, so you use their favorite. This ensures you utilize their preferred platform to maintain their connection. It is incredible how so many women immediately ask what media each uses and instantly connect. It is now their daily social time joy.
- If someone has a generic name, ask them to connect with you first. It's easier than hunting for the specific Mary Smith or Scott Jones.
- Within a short period of starting my consulting business, previous co-workers, neighbors, and vendors were "friends requesting" me, so I did likewise. Here are the exciting observations:
  - People watch you from a distance to visually see what you are doing, yet often won't engage more.
  - Many people will wildly congratulate you on successfully launching a business. Be grateful when congratulated, even if it feels weird since you have not finished completing your adventure.
  - To better understand someone's character and qualities, ask to be introduced by a mutual friend. Either online or in-person, a warm introduction is always preferred.
- People love to respond to posts with enthusiasm even though they act much more restrained in public.

- Some people will be active with you online and never pick up the phone to talk. They prefer to view you from afar, yet they feel genuinely deeply connected to you. Since you don't see who is looking at everything you post, you can be unaware of who is supportive from afar. For example, sometimes, when I bump into a neighbor or friend that I had not seen in a while, they would relate all the fabulous things I had done over the past year in great detail. I could see they were thrilled to see the adventures in my new world. They were raving "secret" fans. Initially, it confused me and made me sad that I had been unaware of how much they treasured our connection. If I'd known they felt that connected with me, I could have reached out. Later I realized they were happy admiring my progress from afar, which was still a form of friendship. It was not my ideal version of a true friendship, but it still was a loving connection. Just because it was virtually connected, it was a friendship to be recognized because they celebrated my journey, and many prayed for my success. That's like our chapter when we discussed the value of having a Prayer Warrior in your friendship circle. Those are powerful and welcome friends indeed!

If you are virtually celebrating someone's success and never reach out, please consider giving them a sign of real encouragement (note or phone call). If you prefer to remain remote, that is fine too. The power of prayer is a perfect way to bless them. Instead, if you talk to someone dealing with significant change, you might be surprised how delighted they are to hear from you. Remember my personal saga when I felt so alone building a new identity and how no one could tell looking at me. A quick voicemail or heartfelt card would have made my heart sing with joy.

Consider a more active form of communication the next time you find yourself following someone's journey. If you reconnect, you might discover they were meant to be your true friend, but you never got the opportunity to let the relationship deepen in the past.

Editing Allows Us to Appear More Likeable in a Virtual World

We've talked about the beauty of using observation as one of your best tools to discern the qualities of a potential friend. For observation purposes, social media is another tool to look at another's world. It's a perfect place to grasp what's happening in their daily life and current interests. For those reasons, I recommend you spend some social media time to further connect with those you've met socially or in business. At the same time, I highly recommend you maintain your awareness. Don't confuse connecting virtually with someone as being the same as an in-person developed friendship. Ideally, we use a mental filter on our words before we speak. Once our words are spoken, however, they float into the air and cannot be edited. We talk and learn how it is received when we see their facial reaction.

In real life, a conversation is much like a tennis game. There is no delete button to hit if we reply to someone with something too transparent, emotional, or hurtful. Being in person or on the phone, we do not have the luxury of carefully crafting our conversation. There is no delete button to backspace our words out of spoken dialogue to appear more likable. The ability to craft and filter a virtual message is why you can't always get an accurate read on a *virtual* friend's qualities.

An audio-based social media platform allows a person's genuineness (good or bad). Why? In an active conversation, we reveal beliefs and values. This transparency is not always the same in virtual written communications. The posts you read are not always the same as what someone stands for. Let's think this through. When we make a post, we review the words typed before we hit send. (Note: If you don't do that, you should.) If we don't like our wording, we can edit our message, ensuring it is scripted to convey what we intended. If we question how someone will interpret our words, we throw in a few emojis 😀 😫 😂 to clarify the message. Once we like how our message flows, we hit SEND. Yet, that's not how real live conversations work. How can we believe most of what is posted, knowing it can be fully edited before being shared? That is an interesting thought to consider, right?

Hybrid Approach

That is why I recommend you consider adopting a hybrid approach when you find yourself ready to deepen a relationship solely maintained online. If you've connected for a while virtually and realize you both genuinely like each other, move it to a video conference or phone call. That allows you both to hear, listen, and respond in a live conversation. Listen to their voice and the words that are chosen when there is no editing ability.

TIP:

Think of social media as your tool to build trust with those interested in knowing more about you. Social media platforms should not be a place where you create an altered version of yourself that is carefully edited and scripted. Think of it as an extension of yourself to showcase the qualities and character others will see in real life. For that reason, I prefer connecting with others on Instagram, LinkedIn, Clubhouse, and YouTube because it lets their personalities shine more transparently. Here is an easy way for you to find me and reach out to say hello, go to https://linktr.ee/theredhawk. That link is called a bio tree. Many bio trees are free, and it allows you to load all your social media links into one easy spot for others to connect.

TIP:

Do not think a friendship grown solely virtually should stay that way forever unless you've decided it is best kept at a distance and casual. If they live in another area, let them know when you are traveling through and offer to meet for coffee or invite them to an event. Great friendships start online, and it is up to us to decide how to evolve the relationship.

Words Have Power – Words Can Confuse – Message with Clarity
As helpful as social media can be to quickly check in with someone to show you care or celebrate them, it can also be so easy that it makes us overly relaxed in keeping friendships. We aim to get closer, and sometimes the opposite happens. When you are not in person, you are limited in your ability to interpret the messages of others by reading words and emojis. Our brains are wired to relate to one another, human to human. The overuse of technology allows too much room for misinterpretation to happen.

Humans need to see faces and hear voices to feel the energy to understand what is shared fully. By limiting our communications to reading someone's words, we restrict our understanding of who is on the other side of the device. Remember, words only carry a 7% effective ability as a communication mode. Audio is 38%, and body language is 55% effective. We need to remind ourselves that our messages can be interpreted differently from what we intend when we type and post. For example, I have witnessed a suffering friend, Fiona, who felt ignored by her online friends. She believed her post clearly explained her level of distress, yet when I read her post, it was not obvious at all. Her post emotions appeared as if she didn't care or was apathetic. So, what happened? Her virtual friends read her post, did not pick up on her pain and minimized her grief about her sudden job loss. That frequently happened during the pandemic. Many people were overwhelmed by their circumstances and stayed in their own "bubbles." Some struggled to express their wide range of emotions clearly. Instead of Fiona's online friends reaching out, they posted supportive cheerful comments. They never dug deeper to comprehend her level of suffering or reached out to her outside of social media. They thought all would be well with Fiona eventually and moved on to read the next post. Fiona felt abandoned online and ignored by her virtual friends and took a hiatus from all posting. Then suddenly, her online friends woke up that something was amiss. They had to reach outside of social media to make contact and ask why she was in despair. See how the virtual world can unknowingly create a sense of confusion in a friendship circle?

Just as in real life, what we do or say virtually can repel another from leaning in to learn more about us. I have witnessed sarcasm in a post construed as cruel by one and thought to be funny by another. Another confusing reaction can happen when others don't "follow" or "friend" us back quickly. If we "friend request" someone we really wanted to meet and finally get brave enough to request connecting, those are the times we can feel especially rejected when they don't immediately respond. Why? Because that person was important to us, and we anticipated a response. It is usual for anyone to consider a lack of response as a potential rejection. Our brains start overthinking why the person chose not to reply or accept our friend request. We follow someone and expect them to follow us back. Yet, we often fail to embrace that it might not be personal.

In many cases, a delay was not intentional. The person failed to respond because they either didn't see our request or had pressing life issues. On LinkedIn, for example, there is an acceptable delay period in accepting a "connect request" because most people will first read your profile, look for mutual connections, then decide if they want to connect. That is considered wise. Not everyone we ask to connect with will decide they want to connect, especially if there are zero mutual connections. We will talk soon about how to intrigue others with your invite to connect every time.

Truths to Consider About the Virtual World and Friendship Making:
- Being curious builds friendships virtually, just like in person. Politely dig deeper with interesting questions (while on social

media) to learn truths about the person's character and beliefs to determine how that aligns with yours.

- Connecting 100% virtual will not allow you the ability to evolve into a true friendship—it should be followed up offline eventually.
- Hearing the voice and tone plus reading body language establishes trust quicker than reading a post.

Beware of Monkey-Mind

Being more engaged virtually can consequently limit our mental ability to be genuinely present. How so? We start a quick post, then comment on someone's post, and "monkey-mind" happens. Like a monkey swinging among trees, we jump from one person to another person's posts. Consequently, the first post we read did not fully get absorbed. Since we are not fully present, distraction quickly happens, and we misread the emotional state of a friend's post. If they don't feel like you are paying full attention, what you write can sound generic, making the emotional connection thin.

Post-COVID Time – The Struggle to Be a *Real Deal* Friend While Distancing

During the pandemic, people felt isolated more than ever and struggled to find ways to keep and be real friends. It was a challenge due to the instant mandate to socially distance, making our primary option more virtual unless we made a phone call. It felt like we were driving on a highway then all known bridges leading to our destinations collapsed. So we had to pull over and sit in our car. Some people called that being in their "own bubble." The introverts embraced the new solitude easier with their innate ability to welcome limited socializing. While extroverts felt lonely and cut off from society and human contact. This is a great time to work on looking for friendships.

- Many people really need a new friend at this moment.
- Following up with those you meet online or virtually in meetings is a great start.

Being Virtual – Opportune Friendships Can Happen When Least Expected

Meeting others online in forums, groups, and clubs can sometimes lead to a surprising, excellent connection. For example, some of my relationships formed on the Clubhouse (audio app) mentioned how using that app to hear someone's voice was a blessing, especially during the pandemic. Why? Because they were able to engage in a real conversation hearing a person's voice even though they were not seen. During the isolation, they felt like they were heard, and attentive listening sparked a friendship. The more they saw the same people in a club and listened to their voices, the more comfortable they openly expressed themselves. Being heard, developing comfortability, and trust to openly talk are crucial elements in any friendship forming. No wonder Clubhouse grew from 1,500 users in May 2020 to 10 million active users by March 1, 2021.

It is possible for an audience to instantly feel a human-to-human connection while in a virtual audio-based club or on a virtual stage. Remember we talked about the power of the human voice? Hearing someone's tone and inflection is 38% effective in communicating the message, whereas written words only carry 7% effectiveness. I was thrilled to hear Clubhouse users remarking they felt that virtual app gave them a place to develop deeper connections.

One lady shared, "I felt like my Clubhouse friends cared more about me and what was going on than my real friends!" That was profound. She had met them in a virtual audio-only app and followed up on an Instagram direct message (DM) to set up a time to talk more on a one-to-one basis. Clearly, it was the follow-ups that cemented their relationships to deepen. These people were not bound by the traditional friendship that grows based on proximity and frequency. It's a whole new mold of friendships being formed virtually.

Another example is how a women's group of 50+ ages has established their own club and set up travel trips to meet in Miami for a girls' weekend. Another club is planning an excursion trip to Tuscany, Italy in 2022 with its members. I imagine by the time that trip happens, they will be true friends dining in the vineyards.

Being Virtual – Etiquette

In the virtual world, when connecting with an acquaintance, or a friend, a different set of etiquette rules are required. The winning approach happens virtually, connecting when you combine etiquette with awareness, discernment, and observation.

Many of these etiquette rules of conduct are the same as when connecting with a stranger in the physical world, but we may have forgotten them because we can become too relaxed when virtual.

- Use the same situational awareness and discernment wisely to consider whether to further discussions with a virtual connection.
- Pace the timings of your posts and follow-ups. Volley the postings like a conversation, much like tennis.
- Be inspiring and enlightening with your posts while still being you.
- If you are having an unusually horrible day, social media may not be the right place to share your emotions. After a while, if you feel compelled to ask for some help or prayers, then make your post. Or if later you have an uplifting story to share how you dealt with that issue, then make your post. It's better to have a "clear head" when posting.
- Be judicial regarding what information you share until you gain another's trust, and they earn your trust.
- Be patient and not overly transparent. Saying too much information about yourself or your private world too early in any relationship can cause a red flag. An acquaintance is considering whether they want to learn more about you as a potential friend.
- Be present and attentive to what others are posting. Remember the story of Fiona. Sometimes what others post may be minimizing their

emotional state. Look deeper and follow up if you sense they are dealing with a challenge or a life change.

- Do not rush a friendship. Let it organically grow.
- Look and assess whether that person fits into your ideal qualities list as a friend. Remember, you are on a journey to *Collect True Friends*, and allow yourself the luxury to only admit those into the inner circle you discerned are a good potential fit. For example, you've posted back and forth over months, and they initially felt like a great person to chat with further. Take the time to see if your instincts were right.
- Before you offer to schedule a Zoom or phone call to hear their voice, look again at their old post to determine their values or qualities.
- Be polite and not "tag" anyone in a post that you haven't developed a great connection with previously. Tagging someone's name in your post that is not emotionally connected with you yet can be interpreted as presumptuous or pushy. It's always best to ask or direct message (DM) asking if you may tag them in explaining why it is important in your world.
- Behave virtually with your messages and posts the same as you would in person. Remember everything you type is public and discoverable later. Therefore, do not say things you wouldn't shout on a megaphone at a picnic of reporters.
- Be you, the "real deal." Do not put on a persona you want others to see. Remember, what we post is usually what others believe, so if you might meet them later, make sure that the virtual person is the real you.
- Embrace follow-up as your new habit. Do this consistently as your secret sauce that builds a deeper connection. It will make you stand out from the crowd.
- Respond timely when someone reaches out. Don't leave them wondering about your delay or thinking you've "ghosted" them.
- Don't always rely on the other person to do the follow-up. Take turns initiating.

- Be mindful of what message or image you publicly share in your posts. For example, your friends may not feel comfortable seeing you have posted their photo without being asked first. Ask your friends if that is alright before including them in your action posts. Some have careers sensitive to social media images shown, or others may prefer privacy and not want to be included in group shot photos.

- Be sensitive about the types of photos you post, especially with others involved. For example, a friend was embarrassed when a co-worker randomly showed up where she was dining, ordered shots of liquor, took a photo, and left her table. Later my friend was tagged in a party photo and worried about her company seeing those colorful photos. She called and asked her co-worker to delete the post.

- Be sensitive that friends could feel left out when you post images of you socializing with other friends. This can happen when they've repeatedly invited you to catch up, and you neglected to set a date or include them in such outings. If you want to meet in smaller social groups, perhaps not post group images or limit your settings to who gets to view them.

TRUTH BOMB:

Some people find "keyboard courage," meaning they will say disturbing things they would not usually reveal about others, events, or weird circumstances. Those red flag moments are vital opportunities to observe and check for your non-negotiables. For example, a non-negotiable for me is someone embracing hatred for groups or using blasphemy. Those things repel me from getting closer. Unknown beliefs may become transparent in someone's posts when their emotions are inflamed.

Follow Up-to Follow Through.

If you want to stand out in the virtual world of friends and connections, remember to note important things are happening with someone you've become interested in. I like to add them to the notes section under their contact info and the date—for example, birthday September 22. Twin kids (Gavin and Grace) are graduating and heading to VCU 2022. She loves orchids. Husband retires in August 2024 from the Navy. To make it easier, set an appointment reminder as an annual event to reach out. This is very helpful with any first's (anniversary or death).

Why is this important? Because as said by President Teddy Roosevelt, *"People don't care how much you know until they know how much you care."'*

Don't Rush the Ask on Social Media – Connect First to Build a Relationship.

The biggest mistake made on social media is saying or asking for something you would never do in person. For example, imagine you are walking outside to water your roses and see your new neighbor. Instead of introducing yourself and welcoming her to the neighborhood, you ask if you can borrow their lawnmower and could they watch your dog next week when you're on vacation. As bizarre as that might sound, that's what people constantly do on Facebook, Instagram, LinkedIn, and email lists. Sadly, that has caused many to be hesitant about connecting with anyone they haven't been mutually introduced to. Caution is wise when asked to accept a friend request from someone unknown or who has zero mutual connections. Our first reaction is curiosity about what made them reach out. Just like the neighbor outside being pursued by favor requests. If you do not know the person walking by and had not seen them before, would you really start asking favors? Of course not. You would approach them, learn something about them, and maybe offer a resource to help them first. Over time your trust would build based on bumping into each other. Trust builds that same way over time on social platforms or virtual rooms (i.e., ZOOM or SKYPE) or Clubhouse (audio app).

The next biggest mistake is to make a connection request and not indicate why you wanted to connect. This applies over the phone, online, and on social media. First, it is ideal to message the person on that app and say, "I see we are both friends with Jackie, and I'd like to connect. I used to live in Phoenix too." That gives the person some context on why you are asking to connect. Here is a Truth Bomb. Many of your friends will accept a connection request if mutual connections exist, yet later remove the received request if the requestor fails to follow up. Why? Because if the requestor wanted a relationship, they'd follow through explaining what prompted them to make a friend or follower request. That is a real belief held by many on social media.

TIP:

Remember, if you make a connection request, state why you'd like to connect. An example of a proper message request is, "It was great to see you were in the same women's group today where we heard my friend Karin Schultz speak on work-life balance. It's nice to meet you. I'd like to connect." That allows the person to accept your request and respond with a conversational point of reference.

TIP:

Never start a virtual message with "How are you?" It's like a stranger walking up to you in the parking lot, looking into your eyes, and asking, "How are you?" It's out of place and doesn't feel comfortable.

Don't Rush the *Trust* Phase into True Friends Phase

Another big mistake when we try to connect over technology is accelerating from the *we just met* phase, *starting to trust*, then leap into *close friends'* phase. This frequently happens in the virtual world and usually makes the other person uncomfortable. It feels the equivalent of this example. Imagine you are in your local grocery store checking out. You start talking to your regular cashier, and she comments about a canned item she's scanning. You ask her about that brand and if she's tried it. It seems like a perfect conversation. Then the cashier hands you a receipt and closes your conversation with, "My family is going away for the weekend; you should come with us."

Ok, how weird did that feel reading that huge jump in familiarity? That's how people overstep virtually when connecting with a "friend" or misread a message like "we should connect with each other." Trust between you both needs time to organically happen. Just because you've seen someone frequently does not mean they know you. It's like making hot tea. Trust needs time to brew and steep. When trust hasn't been allowed ample time, it feels contrived or suspicious as discussed in the earlier chapter, which triggers a friendship roadblock.

Emotional Collateral
Emotional collateral is the substance between two people or a group of friends who have shared time together. It develops when volunteering, sporting, partying, dining, working on a project, etc. This gets us to the next level by fostering trust. The potential for building trust increases as the age of the relationships grows more profound and the more often we see each other. This requires that we open up to others around us. We must be the real deal for others to get to learn more about us. For example, when I am in a group, I sport a sense of humor with quirky positivism to bring joy to those around me. As an extrovert, I think it is much easier to build emotional collateral with others by being in person. Many of my introverted friends say it's easier for them to do it by connecting virtually. This is excellent news for an introvert. If someone truly likes them online, it will be an even deeper connection made if they later meet in person.

Also, work to build emotional collateral with your social media friends. If you say or do something slightly weird, there is enough collateral exchanged those others will overlook the poor judgment. Spend the time layering your messaging so others gain a truthful view of who you are as you keep striving to be the best version of a true friend. Solid trust with your online connections is what keeps a relationship engaged. When someone doesn't have enough ties "collateral" in our emotional friendship reservoir, they cannot blindly show up and start asking favors. This is especially true when we haven't heard from a friend in a while, so they aren't aware of all the challenges we've been handling. This is a universal concept amongst all age groups (Millennials, Gen-X, Gen-Z, and Baby Boomers). No one overlooks a takers' rude behavior.

TRUTH BOMB:

Having poor judgment in posting things that upset others is only recoverable when you have enough emotional collateral with your followers and friends. Otherwise, when there is no emotional bond between you, they might unfriend you.

 PONDERING PAUSE:

- Can you recall when you virtually joined a social media group (or event) and felt awkward?
- Did it seem like everyone belonged there more than you?
- Did someone attempt to help you feel more comfortable with the environment?
- If no one acted welcoming to you, are you sure you appear approachable to others?
- What did you wish someone had done differently to make you feel less awkward virtually attending?
- If you virtually meet someone today, what will you do to make them feel more welcome connecting to you? What will you do to make them want to learn about you?

Reminders: Whether in person or online, you first must know someone, like them, then you get to the trust. When trust hasn't been built over an appropriate amount of time, we find ourselves feeling disturbed. We usually don't realize at first why we feel unsettled. It's more like a feeling in our gut alarming us that something is rushing at us, and this person might harm us. Notice that trust must develop over an "appropriate time" because the time requirements vary based on who we meet. Sometimes there is an instant connection that quickens our trust. That can happen, especially when someone else is in another friend's inner circle. However, trust takes longer to gain, especially connecting virtually, when we have little or no background about an acquaintance or colleague. In that situation, a friendship needs time to evolve on its own appropriate timeline.

Since you are developing a mindset to *Collect True Friends* throughout your life, make it an ultimate goal to be aware of friendship opportunities everywhere, especially during periods of separation, disaster, or forced distance. As we've seen, being virtually and emotionally connected helped us survive isolation imposed from long-time distancing. Remember, frequency fosters a more profound connection, whether in person or online.

Now let's walk through a few unique ways to reach out to others virtually or from a social distance. You may want to adopt a few of these into your everyday routines:

- Schedule a monthly Sunday video conference call with a group of your friends scattered across the world. It might seem a little awkward until they learn more about each other. Then once they become engaged, you'll enjoy watching the conversations spark.
- Schedule a regular religious study or book club study to discuss a common read.
- I like the app called "Marco Polo" with a small group of good friends to record a quick instant message with a video. This increases your frequency of communicating, and messages can be retrieved later.

It's perfect for busy lifestyles allowing you to open a message when you are available. That way, when you do finally see each other as a group, you are already caught up on life's happenings, and your time together is richer.

- Schedule outdoor dates to kayak, hike, beach, shop at a farmers' market, cook a new recipe, or tour a museum's gardens.
- Schedule a standing time to meet to walk a path. This is ideal to do before your workday begins or on lunch. Try twice a week to catch up on what's happening while you get in your exercise. My dear friend Terri and I have walked routinely for years to sandwich in exercise with catching up.
- Schedule a work party for a community project. Invite friends to bring gloves and tools and catch up while making a positive difference, like my friend, Martha.

You've now discovered how different it is making and keeping friends online than in person. Many benefits, as well as challenges, exist; connecting virtually and developing the relationships takes time and skill. You've also gathered tools to navigate your messaging for posting and commenting effectively. Especially helpful to retain is the information about staying in touch if someone relocates or anytime that social distancing is required in life. This provides your next foundation step as you climb the flight of steps to becoming a true friend whom others will seek. Our next chapter will explore how to be "the real deal" when connecting so that you earn quality friends worthy of your time and devotion.

CHAPTER 7

HOW TO BE A MAGNET TO TRUE FRIENDS
– BE THE REAL DEAL

WHEW! Having many relationships, people often ask me, "Elizabeth, you know so many people—doesn't it exhaust you to have all those people in your life?" I've pondered that question a lot. This is what I know as truth. If you have too many of the wrong relationships, then *yes*, it would be exhausting. Sometimes it can seem like we have *too* many people in our lives that we don't want to spend time with (like weird co-workers or fake friends) and yet not enough quality people (true friends). It's a lot like when we discussed that a volume of virtual online friends is not the same as in-person true friends. Social media can provide a fun place to respond to dozens of posts daily, yet we wonder who truly listens. In essence, you can feel alone standing in a crowd of people.

Have you ever felt that way? That's when having too many people in your life doesn't feel right. That's because it's not the right tribe for you, or perhaps you've outgrown that set of friends. So, answering the question, it is not exhausting to be connected to a high volume of true friends who return your energy. It can infuse more life into your soul. Healthcare studies show those with deeper quality friendships live longer and stay happier. That's another great incentive to your efforts into becoming the "real deal" version of a true friend. Remember, like attracts like.

The second most asked question I get is, "How can I attract better people in my life?" I tell them about my *Three Big Ws*. If these resonate with you as a strong fit, feel free to adopt them for your own. If another one pops into your mind, consider it as well. I suggest you take some time to reflect and nail down your answers to these three Ws as your foundational start to being the "real deal" true friend.

Here are the Three Big Ws:

Who Are You? You determine this by recognizing your non-negotiables. For example, my non-negotiable is mean people or gossipers. They don't get invited into my inner circle (business or personal), and I strive to steer clear of those types. I meet more people professionally than socially, so I created the protective mantra "*I Seek Meaningful Work with Nice People*" to ensure I attract quality people. It helps God send me those that I am supposed to meet and hopefully repel any mean-spirited people.

What Do You Stand For? I like to attract wholesome people who want to help others and use logic to reason. Being a person of faith makes it easier to connect because it acts as a lighthouse beacon. It is like we automatically understand how important faith is in everything pursued or accepted. I also stand for encouraging everyone to use their minds. I run from group thinkers and strive to be surrounded by people smarter than me.

My goal is to gravitate towards those who critically think for themselves and act kindly to others. I'm sure my *Little Viking Girl* experiences imprinted my attraction towards such people. You, too, have core values imprinted. When you highlight these, you shine like the "real deal" in friendships. Your values need to be recognized and proclaimed as what you stand for. You cannot be wishy-washy on your core values, or else you stand for nothing. We've all heard the phrase "*those who stand for nothing will fall for anything.*" To *Collect True Friends* into your life with the qualities you desire to have more of, you must choose your values and behaviors. To help gain more clarity on what you stand for, ask yourself:
- What is the thing I want to be known for when my time is up?
- What actions do I want others to remember I regularly do?
- What is my legacy?

Who Is Your Tribe? To help gain more clarity, ask yourself:

- Who are the types of people that uplift me, inspire me, and want me to be all I can be?
- How do I feel when I am with those types of uplifting friends?
- Who are the people I've met that genuinely want to see me achieve more and push me forward?
- Who are those people? (Write names.)
- Have I been to a place where I felt interesting, stimulating, and comfortable even though I could not say precisely why? (*Listen to your subconscious.*)
- Where are these people hanging out? Write down that place to remember later because they are my tribe.

If I Don't Like the Vibe, They are Not My Tribe!

If people you've always known, lived near, worked with, or regularly see are not aligned with your three Ws, it's time to consider where they differ. I like to say, "*If I don't like the vibe, they're not my tribe!*" Remember when we were young, and our mothers told us to be careful about choosing friends we hang out with? It applies as we grow up—the people surrounding us affect when, if, and how we develop. As children, we formed most of our friendships in school. However, adult friendships are made in various areas, especially after work hours—at the fitness club, church, parties, charity, sports, hobbies, neighborhood, etc. I encourage you to rethink the locations where you will meet more of your ideal types of people (your tribe). If you are still unsure what places they might frequent, revert to your qualities list previously created. Peek at the traits and types of people you want more of in your inner circle. Use that knowledge to re-energize your focus to find more of your tribe, tying it back to those interests. Bump that list up against where you previously met an ideal inner circle friend. That is your perfect environment potentially to meet more of your tribe.

So is asking your inner circle for introductions to their friends with the traits you listed.

So those are my Three Big Ws: Who are you? What do you stand for? Who is your tribe? Did you add another to your Ws list? Remember, our goal is to get you to be the "real deal" worthy of someone's time and devotion level. Where your true friendship skills are today is a beginning. They will continue to evolve if you stay committed to your development. Working your way through this book is a perfect example of such commitment. You are here because you want to maximize your positives and let go of what actions served you poorly in past friendships. An effective way to fine-tune your friendship-making skills is by using the powers of observation. Observing how others act helps you model what behaviors to embrace or stop.

How to Become a Huge Observer

To find out someone's genuine character and not be fooled, it is best to notice from a distance how they interact with others. It is easy to practice observation when standing in line to get your coffee. For example, notice how strangers look at each other. Did they appear warm and approachable to those they did not know? Did they acknowledge you were there in the same area or looked away? Who was friendly only to whom they were meeting? I love to watch how others react out of their comfort zone. It gives vital information to calculate how that person handles stressful situations. Great examples could be how the person reacts when giving the wrong change, is made to wait in a long line, or handle someone struggling to open a door. How someone is treating you and others screams volumes of information. When observing them from a distance, use your awareness and discernment skills; we've been working on considering that person for friendship.

How To Authentically Deepen Your Connection – Be the Real Deal

Isn't it a fabulous feeling when you finally have a great conversation with a stranger? If I've had a great conversation with someone, I let them know they made a favorable impression and that I would like to know them better. That may sound simple enough. Yet surprisingly, few people do this. Instead, they are reluctant to be the first ones to suggest getting together again. What happens when we forget to express why the other person made such a great impression? Nothing. That is the problem. The person has no idea why you are drawn to talk more and may not sense the common connection.

TIP:

Five Friendship bonding techniques
- Immediately let them know you would like to stay in touch.
- Mention precisely how they made a good impression.
- Ask for the best way to follow up.
- Exchange your phone numbers or business cards (if they have one).
- If they seem inviting, propose a quick lunch or coffee date. Tell them you will call later in the week to confirm.

To be the real deal, use those fundamental bonding tips when starting a friendship. If these are new to you and you want to feel comfortable applying them next time, here's an easy thing to do. Observe how others are using those five bonding tips and watch them in action. Your goal is then to embrace the qualities or actions you most admire in others. Modeling the behavior of someone who engages well with others makes applying these new skills easier. If you think about it, that's what we did as kids. We'd watch how someone older and proficient did something and copied their movements. Now that you've learned the five friendship bonding techniques, you will recognize when others use them.

Be Genuine and Bold with Your Follow Up – Be the "Real Deal"
Taking the bold step to ask the person to talk further is the most overlooked step in friendship making. Why? Because the other person thinks if you wanted to know them better, you would have asked. What? How can that be? That makes no sense. Yet, it's true, and it frequently

happens, particularly among reserved people. So, if two people meet, have a great conversation, and neither one is bold enough to initiate a follow-up date, guess what happens? Nothing. The friendship never gets any chance to see if it should bloom. Sometimes you have to keep running into the same person over and over until both people get the agreed confirmation; they like each other. Then finally, one is admitting they'd like to talk more. That's what I call a bold and genuine request.

The Secret to *Collecting True Friends*

If you are going to attract amazing quality people into your world, you have to be willing to be the one to ask to see someone in the future. You have to be the one who tells them why they made such a great impression. Waiting for everyone else to take action will limit your choices for friendships. The great thing is you won't always be the initiator. One day you will run into someone you mutually like, and they will beat you to the question and say, "Want to grab a coffee sometime?" When this happens, smile, realizing they made the bold move to collect a friend and show them your appreciation.

Follow Up – What Works Best – To Be the "Real Deal"

If your time is limited and you are unsure about driving a distance, go virtual using ZOOM or Facetime. Or fit in a phone call. Your goal is to hear their voice and ideally see their face which optimizes connecting. Why? Because 38% of our communication ability flows vocally, and 55% comes from body language.

You will be shocked how adding the ability to see and hear someone turns a causal connection into a true friend. Texting and emailing does not warm the soul enough. Follow-up is critical in learning more about potential friends. It's only a small investment of your time, and you might realize you were correct, and this is a beautiful person to know. Or if not, you still might learn something useful. If you discover they are not what you thought, not your cup of tea, at least you made an effort. Nothing ventured, nothing gained!

Learn About the Person You Plan to See Again – Make an Effort – Be Curious

It's essential to make an effort to understand the person you'd like to know better. Ideally, it is best to find out what their likes are or what they are known for in their world. They might be an author, community leader or chess wizard as an example. You are trying to identify their non-negotiables, what they stand for, and who their tribe is. You can even google people's names and be amazed to learn all the places they lived before and what they were into. How cool would it be if you once lived in the same places? Social media has made information gathering much easier, and we are all accustomed to looking at profiles. It is helpful to know if you have any mutual connections. If convenient, ask one of your mutual connections what activity they enjoy doing with that person. So please take a few moments before you see them again and look them up (i.e., Instagram, Linked-in, Facebook, YouTube, TikTok, Twitter, Clubhouse).

In-person events are ideal for observing how that person engages with one of your friends. Be curious in a genuinely nice way to learn more about their connection. For example, you could ask your friend, "Hey Abigail. I noticed you've been talking with Veronica. How do you know each other?" Having such knowledge helps you identify common interests and mutual friends before your next time together. The cool part is this can spark the idea for several of you to make plans together.

Vetting is a Good Thing

So back to the beauty of using observation as your new interpersonal skill. I can't stress this enough. If possible, try to watch them interact with others. See how they treat people. Doing a little observation and social media research is a smart strategy. Successful people regularly use it before they openly let someone near their inner circle. It's called vetting. Asking others what they know of the person's interest or background, plus how they met, helps you assess their character. A conversation with a mutual friend is a perfect opportunity to name-drop and observe the response. You could also mention what fascinated you about that person and listen for common interests. It might turn out the three of you are all interested in an upcoming concert or sporting event that can widen the friendship circle. However, occasionally you might hear negative feedback. If this happens, I recommend you steer clear of gossip. Be kind and gracious with information relayed. You are asking for helpful facts about the mutually known person. Share what you know, not what you heard. Be observant, do a little research, and politely ask others for their tidbits. Those tips improve your opportunities to befriend people who best fit in your world. Believe me when I tell you, vetting can save you time, money, and angst. Your focus is to find more of those who might match your three Ws (who you are, what you stand for, who your tribe is).

Watching and Being Watched – Be the "Real Deal"
Before mixing them into your world, knowing someone's real nature can also save you frustration and possible embarrassment. For example, observe how they treat the waitress, receptionist, kids, animals, or parking lot attendant. Their real character is revealed when they think the world is not watching. Keep in mind that while you are focused on attracting more quality people into your life, you are also protecting yourself. To gain people's trust, they must observe you being the real deal. What you do or say directly affects who wants to be your friend.

 PONDERING PAUSE

Here are some questions to consider when assessing how others may see you:

- Do I consistently model the best version of myself? Even alone?
- Do I engage others (act inclusive) around me in the circle of discussion?
- Do I exclude others around me in conversations?

- Recently, when talking with someone new, was I able to establish an initial level of trust?
- Do I consistently and genuinely compliment people I meet?
- At my last gathering, how many people can I remember complimenting?
- What did someone compliment me on?
- How do I feel strangers usually react when meeting me?
- Do others take an interest in my conversation?
- Do they draw closer to me to hear more (like a magnet)?
- Do they step back and find a reason to distance themselves?
- If they withdraw, was it the topic or possibly my handling of the topic?
- Could I have been too intense, self-engaged, or offensive in any way?
- Do I let them talk enough and listen to what they say?
- Do I pace my replies during the conversation, speak too little, or take over?
- Do others usually ask to see me again?
- What should I do more of so others want to see me again?

Focus Your Energy on the Other Person – Be the "Real Deal"
One of the easiest and kindest ways to make a new friend is to show genuine interest, ask them a question, and stop to listen to their reply. I've met many people who initially appeared likable yet sadly were later revealed to be solely absorbed with their interests. They never really noticed the person standing in front of them or how others saw them. They saw themselves as delightful and charming. In truth, they were boring and overbearing. So they collected short-term friends who were drawn to them more as a curiosity and then later peel off when their true character was revealed.

A good conversation is like playing tennis. All players must be involved. Keep it flowing, but don't try to score too many points. If you are the dominant personality, make an effort to encourage the other person to talk. They will appreciate and remember your kindness. We discussed that technique when we covered the differences between introverts and extroverts. Remember, the introverts are patiently waiting their turn to speak. Their words are likely to be fascinating because they have taken the time to think before they speak.

Conversely, extroverts immediately say what is on their minds while thinking aloud. That is why extroverts may seem indecisive because they appear to change their minds. In reality, they are forming an opinion. Introverts do the same thing but not aloud. Focusing your complete energy on the other person during a conversation makes you stand out in the crowd. Allowing the other person to participate in the conversation will make you memorable to that person.

Egocentric people rarely learn details about others unless it is something of interest in *their* world. Hopefully, such people's intentions quickly become apparent. Those self-absorbed people ignore social clues and do not realize their behavior is unwelcome. Selfish people fail to see, among other things, the harm they do by focusing only on themselves. They could choose to make the conversation fun and memorable, but instead, they make it a lecture. Paying attention to the person nearby is such a small act of kindness, but it can make a big difference in that person's day. You might be the only person who said a kind word to them that week. Recently, I reminded an acquaintance that she was doing God's work, and others greatly appreciated it. She looked at me, stunned, and I could tell she appreciated the affirmation of kindness. Moments like that can lay a foundation for future friendships.

Curious People Make Friends Easier – Be the "Real Deal"
Making and collecting true friends and building meaningful relationships requires a genuine interest in others. Being genuinely interested to hear more about someone new in your life is not the same as being nosy. Asking thoughtful questions, nodding to their answers, and making an effort to remember what they said are qualities everyone desires in a friend. It's what makes a superficial person stand out from

the real deal person. When we were young, we had an endless curiosity about people and things—everything in our world was new. However, many were convinced by their parents to stop asking questions at an early age. They were told it was considered rude. One acquaintance shared that she'd been told. "Quit asking so many questions, and besides, nobody wants to hear what you have to say." Those stifling parental beliefs train young minds not to be overly interested or curious when meeting others. This is more common than most of us realize. I've met hundreds of people suffering from this misbelief, which limited their success at networking or openly promoting their business. The same happens socially, mixing with others. If we believe we should not dig deeper to learn more about someone, then a friendship cannot grow. The more you practice asking interesting questions, the sooner you become comfortable asking more. Plus, the quality of your questions improves. If you are not comfortable asking a direct question, try eliciting a response. You could say something like, "I bet you have some interesting lessons learned about that." or "That is interesting. There must have been something that compelled you to start that hobby."

Be Open to the Conversation

When someone asks you a thoughtful or heartfelt question, pause, smile, and remember they could be practicing how to better engage in conversations. They may not ask the best questions since they don't know your history. They may look awkward, too, because they are out of their comfort zone, attempting to connect with you. Why? Because being inquisitive is out of their character. If you can respond to questions with grace and maybe ask a few questions in return, it shows you are open to a conversation. Remember, a great conversation is like a friendly game of tennis. From my experience, those conversations build confidence and trust quicker because someone was kind and open enough to respond. The people you were open to speak with might pleasantly surprise you as possessing the qualities on your desired list. How cool would that be?

The curious person is the one who asks questions and shows a genuine interest in what someone else thinks or regards as important. I admit it can feel difficult sometimes when talking with someone who's polar to your interests. I've been in some strange topic conversations where I had no clue about that interest before and probably would never have read about it. However, if you search deep enough while talking, you might find some part of their interests fascinating. Ideal questions might be, "How did you get drawn into this activity? Do you have many friends that enjoy this too?"

Remembering details the person shared, is an excellent way of showing you are interested in seeing them again. You'd be surprised how asking simple questions like, "How was your son's graduation party? Were your relatives able to come to town like you hoped?" pulls them closer. Asking specific questions feeds you ideal details to weave into a later conversation. Plus, it is good manners and makes you stand out in a crowd. If they don't know or like you yet, they will smile and comment on your fabulous memory, then warm up to answer your thoughtful questions. That is the foundation where trust starts to build.

Noting Details – Friendship Making Technique

If you struggle with remembering conversations, make notes under that person's contact on your phone. Conversation notes could include pet and family names, interests, and significant events past or future as well as anniversaries, deaths, births, weddings, promotions, or job changes. Remember this truth. If it is something you'd find important in your life, it would be important to them. They will be pleased you considered those things worth remembering, especially if it is a difficult time like a loss. For example, stopping to send a card, call, or text asking how someone is doing with Mom's Day approaching shows you've remembered they still miss their mother.

What Works Best When Having a Conversation – Be the "Real Deal"

Self-checking our behavior is an ongoing necessity. You can't fix what holds you back from moving forward if you are unaware of it. Growth comes when you can pause and recognize weak areas to concentrate on improvement. For example, as an extrovert who loves to story-tell and hear others laugh, I admit that I can get too animated on occasion when instead I should elicit others to speak more. To correct this conversational behavior, I've had to study new ways of active listening and make an effort to practice. Is it easy to fix a bad conversation habit? No, it's work, and I constantly have to self-check. However, I am determined to improve, and self-checking is part of that process. When I stop talking, I can hear more from the quiet-natured person. Later in this book, we will do an exercise on boosting your active listening skills. So what is something you do during conversations that you wish you could improve? For example, make better eye contact, not fidget, speak slower, speak less, listen more, stand up straighter, ask questions, remember names, laugh more, and understand sarcasm.

Why Self-Check is Necessary to Improve Conversational Abilities

One of my memorable awkward social-mixing moments was trying to help a boisterous young man we will call Ray. He loved to talk and join in every conversation. Unfortunately, Ray only wanted to talk about his life. I tried to change his focus by mentioning interesting things about other people in the ongoing discussion. Bob just returned from Scotland, Ted loves to speed boat, Pamela loves to play golf, Alice is a gourmet cook, and so on. I hoped that Ray would take an interest in something other than himself. To my disappointment and his loss, Ray never once asked anyone anything. Instead, he loudly droned on and on about his fishing trip and the many ways it could have been better. Ray had his monologue and thought others enjoyed it because they stood there. He thought people were interested and engaged when they were really just being polite. When they finally drifted away, Ray leaned over and asked me what I did for a living. At last, I thought, he asked someone a question. I told him I was a consultant and how I love to help people build great relationships by networking better with others.

He smirked, patted me on the back, and said, "Well, it's a good thing I know how to talk to others and don't need any training." Ray's words echoed in my ears. He said, "I know how to talk *to* others." Yet he didn't.

Notice that Ray did not say, I know how to talk *with* others. That one little word demonstrated his lack of self-awareness and (in my quick assessment) any desire to improve further. At that point, I smiled and walked away. Ray moved onto the next group of people who would listen to his tales.

I share this story to emphasize the importance of self-checking and using your awareness skills as a prerequisite to *Collect True Friends* in life. A lack of self-awareness can make it impossible to develop meaningful relationships, professional or personal. Being self-aware is integral to survival. It allows us to assess how we act, adjust course when needed, and evolve into a better, wiser version as we age. When not applied, it can be a roadblock to meeting friends. Just like in Ray's life.

Test if You Are Self-Aware Enough When Connecting with Others
Making time for reflection on how well you are connecting with others is a valuable investment. Here is what to do when reflecting.

 EXERCISE:

- Look at your calendar to schedule a time, ideally when rested, to take a hard look at yourself and determine specific ways you want to improve when meeting or talking with others.
- If you are coming up empty on ways to improve, you might ask your trusted partner or closest long-time friend to share honest

and helpful ways you can be better at conversations. It is not recommended to ask anyone that has a negative, critical attitude.

- Seek input from someone who will speak the truth in a loving, supportive way regarding areas of improvement.
- Ask for specific examples of times when you could have done better to remember the moment more clearly. It is hard to change behaviors if you do not recall doing them. There may have been times you were unaware of your actions being less favorably received by others. A real friend will gently share such information, so welcome the truth and don't shoot the messenger.
- Once you remember a moment, imagine the outcome if you had reacted using your new self-awareness skills. What would you change?
- If your reflection reveals your current mannerisms or behaviors are surprisingly less than ideal, I recommend taking bold action. List them and pick one to fix.
- Write down how you will act in the future, starting today. For example, if you are a non-stop talker, write down, "I will actively listen to the person in front of me and speak 50% less about myself."
- Post that shortlist in several prominent places. My list is posted in my medicine cabinet and over the visor in my car. Give yourself an initial score on these traits. Use any measuring system you like: One-to-ten, Stars, Hearts, etc.
- Remind yourself of the changes you want to make. Every time you see the list, recite those items out loud so your brain can hear you say it. Studies show that *reading words alone* does not have the same impact as *hearing words.*
- Reflect and practice throughout the day. At least three times daily.

Once you've identified the conversation or behavioral areas to improve and formed the habit of repeating them aloud (at least three times a day), it's time to practice in person with a stranger or new friend. I like to try this with people waiting in a doctor's office or salon. They are a captive audience and usually willing to chat to fill the time. For example, if you want to be more patient and interrupt less when speaking, target a friendly appearing person who seems comfortable talking. See how much you can learn about their day or week without interrupting their flow. Count how many times you cut them off in a sentence. Then next time, aim for less with another person.

Perform another self-assessment in thirty days to see how your self-awareness increased. Ironically, at this stage, it really is all about you. Score your performance again and compare it to your previous score. Hopefully, you improved. This is a perfect opportunity to ask for a blessing to help you with your personal development quest. Remember to be specific when asking for help on which behavior you'd want to possess in the future. Don't dwell on the negatives.

Here is Your Advanced Challenge. Ready?
Think about a time when you met someone and later wished you had acted differently. If the person's vibe was generally pleasant and you think they'd be open, reach out to that person and tell them you would like to talk to them again for a few moments. Explain that you are working on your self-awareness training to better connect with others in the future. Share your personal goal on what you are trying to improve upon this year. If they are a kind person and curious, they will be willing to assist you in your growth. If they cannot be available, move on to another.

Here is a story to illustrate how this advanced challenge is done. Years ago, I realized that I failed to notice that my relative was feeling a wide range of emotions over the death of her stepfather. I thought poorly of the man and thought her world would not be significantly affected since he'd been absent for so long. I was mistaken. Even though he was not a good father figure in her life, she grieved and remembered happier days from her early childhood. Her conflicting emotional struggle finally dawned on me when I read her social media posts and felt her pain. I did a self-check and became *aware of how insensitive* I had been by failing to acknowledge the death more sympathetically. I texted to confirm a time to stop by to bring her family a little something. As we stood on her porch and I looked into her eyes, I could see her sorrow. I started with, "There is something I want to apologize for and will try to do better in the future, May I share it with you? "She nodded, and I continued. "When you told me your stepfather had died, my words were too direct and not sympathetic enough. How are you doing now with his death?"

I could see her lean in closer and tilt her head as she let out a deep breath. She felt my sincere acknowledgment of her incredible range of emotions. Then she thanked me for the sympathy card sent and smiled. She gazed peacefully at me, appreciating that I was now aware of how her stepdad's death caused confusion mixed with grief.

Doing a self-check allows you the opportunity to work on future conversation skills in a similar situation. Being the "real deal," a true friend also extends to your family. So many times, we forget to give family members the same space and grace, especially when we don't understand their range of emotions. We expect a family member to respond in a certain way and get upset or surprised when it is contrary. Since we expect a different reaction, we appear uncomfortable or judgmental. Perhaps it's because we don't view family members as friends because they have a different status. Consequently, we can be remiss in giving abundant grace to their suffering. That is a perfect opportunity to be a true friend and act as their Prayer Warrior, mentor, or resource. If in doubt about what to do or say, pray for peace in their aching hearts, their dreams to become peaceful, and their sorrow to heal.

Recap – Identify Your Three Big "W" Questions to Be the Real Deal True Friend

- Who are you?
- What do you stand for?
- Who is your tribe?

Whatever you are doing in your daily life (worker, student, parent, nurse, leader, business owner, officer, teacher, engineer, charity supporter, and the like), identifying the three Ws for yourself will help define who you are. That, in turn, helps determine who you want more of in your world. You've learned how awareness, discernment, and observation are your best skills to build your inner circle. Striving to keep an open mind in your conversations will help you spot more of your potential tribe. Use these skills in your work life, home life, and as you search to *Collect True Friends*. We talked a lot about the power of observation and how helpful this tool will be to find the ones you seek. Don't forget you are constantly being observed. Others are watching to decide if they want to know you better.

Remember to use your list of traits and qualities developed in Chapter 3, so you stay keenly aware of what you want to attract. Your "tribe" has a similar list and is looking for you too. Look for varied people, as discussed in Chapter 4 to fill your inventory (the inner circle) with what is missing. Birds of a feather may flock together, but your tribe can include a variety of people, interests, looks, accents, and backgrounds. You don't have to be or sound like the same bird.

You might already feel it in your heart about which interpersonal areas are holding you back from relating effectively with others. That awareness is a great place to start and commit the time to work on improvement. For many of us, communicating with more clarity and grace is one area to fine-tune. Since you are now on this journey, it is the perfect time to practice using conversational skills we've covered. Why now? Because carrying on a conversation is organically crucial to moving an acquaintance into a friendship. At this point, you have completed the self-awareness exercise to improve conversations with others. Your goal is to practice daily. It takes months for something to become a habit, and frequency will remove any awkwardness or discomfort. Over time with practice, others will welcome you more into conversations and engage longer. Lastly, you've learned the necessity to ask interesting questions and then weave details from previous discussions into conversations. That technique is a sure way to build friendships by showing that you listened, are curious, and genuinely interested. Those qualities roll up to make you the "real deal," which increases your magnetism. Remember, your goal is to attract more people sharing the same values, traits, and qualities. That's why establishing your three Ws is so vital.

When you know in your soul what your non-negotiables are and who you are, then you can easily spot a potential tribe member. For example, givers can spot one another from a distance. There is an air about them of confidence and acceptance based on love for humankind. They even say specific phrases that declare in a non-judgment way who they are and what they stand for. For example, when you ask a giver, "How are you doing?" many will smile and say, "Highly favored, and how are you?" or "I am blessed by the best! How are you doing?" if they are bolder with their faith.

As You Move Forward Being The "Real Deal"
Your daily goal is to be the real deal and observe others to determine who they truly are.

You will become a magnet to others, but you must use your discernment skills to identify which are suitable and which are not for your tribe. As we move on, we will take a deep dive into how to assess when you no longer fit into a tribe or group. In addition, we will explore how to handle friendships with an expiration date even when you failed to notice the friendship faded. Plus, we will discuss declining friendships and ways to exit a dying friendship in the upcoming Dreaded Death of a Friendship chapter.

CHAPTER 8
DREADED DEATH OF A FRIENDSHIP

Adding and removing friends in your inner circle is like tending a friendship garden. Seeding, cultivating, weeding, and nurturing are part of that process, and if you do these things consistently, friendships grow. One of my friends mentioned she had lost several friends because "our lives don't overlap anymore since I quit the martial arts, and we aren't alone on the mat." So, whether we plan to do maintenance on our inner circle or the need to exit is forced upon us, it is an important process that deserves our attention. The key is to know when changes or updates are necessary. When a friendship must end, it is best done with great compassion and sensitivity to those it affects. The death of a friendship can be devastating, much like a romance ending, because you feel the same sense of loss. Something familiar is terminated, and you both realize you will no longer spend time together. It's even sadder when one friend is unprepared for the death of a friendship.

Fortunately, when talking about the death of friendship, we aren't talking about gathering our friends, putting them on an iceberg, shoving them off, and waving goodbye. Whatever term you prefer for letting go of a friend, breaking up, drifting away, or pruning, it ends a relationship. If you shared terrific things in the past and the ending is your idea, being wise and kind is the right thing to do when exiting. If it is not your idea, you may have no choice in the matter. Either way, it is a difficult and painful part of any relationship requiring care to those affected and time for emotional recovery.

Why Some Friendships Should End but Don't End Soon Enough
Being preoccupied or living in denial about a friendship that has been dying on the vine for a while are typical reasons why most of us don't say "enough is enough." We fail to park ourselves long enough to think through if a friendship should continue. Remember, we talked about the

woman carrying around a heavy handbag filled with a mixture of important items and forgotten things? We can get so preoccupied or just accustomed to those in our lives that we occasionally forget to *dump out the handbag* to review the contents and question their value. Instead, something so egregious has to happen that we are finally forced to admit there is a problem. We may realize the problem should have been addressed earlier. That can be the saddest of situations when we get pushed into finally seeing something we long ignored or were just blind to see in our friendship. Clearly, not all friendships are to last forever and that is a harsh reality. However, it is vital to your health and happiness occasionally to look at the levels of your satisfaction with people in your inner circle. Doing the same introspect can help reduce the chance you will be the friend pushed away.

In Chapter 2, we focused on gaining your inner skills (awareness and discernment) about the people we encounter and consider for friendships. In Chapters 3 and 4, we looked at who surrounds you and assessed if they were still a good fit in your inner circle using your desired qualities or traits list. You evaluated your inventory of friends while considering the traits you wanted more of in your inner circle and decided if you needed to find more variety. That open mindset should allow you now the freedom to bring in different types of friends who will enrich your life. When you completed the reflection exercises to define what you want more of in your inventory of friends, a few names may have come to mind.

Here is an exercise I recommend boosting clarity when you find yourself debating or delaying seeing a friend. Choose a time when you are rested. This should take about 15 minutes. If possible, detach from technology and be outdoors to remove all distractions. Open your heart and mind. Remember, you have the answers inside and, with a quiet mind, can hear them. You just need to accept what pops up.

A CONTEMPLATION EXERCISE:

- Grab a favorite beverage. Sipping something you enjoy allows your body to relax while giving yourself a moment to reflect on how you feel.
- Head outside or to your quiet area and as you sip your drink, take two deep breaths.
- Start with asking for assistance in gaining clarity about a certain person. (I like to say a quick prayer, "God, show me the way, bring the clarity I seek into my thoughts and heart.")
- Say the person's name aloud and reflect upon the last few times spent together. Let those memories of times spent together bubble up as emotions.
- Name aloud those emotions you are feeling from the memories. (confused, drained, sorrow, anxious, energy, distanced, regret, drama, jealousy, etc.)
- Name things you liked about your time together (mutual trust, laughter, it is fun, comfortable, easy, we understand each other, accept who we are, and enjoy the same things.)
- Now, the final step. Ask yourself these two questions and answer out loud. Be honest.
  - "Does seeing (insert the person's name) bring me joy or value in my life?"
  - "Do I look forward to seeing (insert the person's name) again?
- Now, pause to reflect what emotions, feelings, and words bubbled up about that person.

If you still feel uncertain about what you want to do next with your friendship, wait a few days. Let your brain and heart clear. Then if a few days later you believe it makes sense, set up a time for an in-person visit (or phone call) to refresh how it feels being together. Now that your awareness is tuned up, seeing, or hearing that friend again will give you emotional validation. Before you meet, remind yourself of those emotions you felt during the exercise. Remind yourself of what you said

144

aloud and how your heart felt. Your goal is objectively to confirm if the emotions and logic felt were temporary or have been brewing. No action is required at this point. You are just in a private discovery phase right now. Do not tell your friend any of those findings or initial thoughts. You need time to sort out in your head and heart what you'd like to say later. We will be discussing how to handle that coming up.

When I Almost Killed Our Friendship - I Blew it Meeting Rosa's Other Best Friend

What a disaster of a night. If only I had known then what I know now. It was a painful lesson to admit how I blew it as Rosa's close friend. I was a college graduate and a first-time homeowner struggling to survive being on my own. My dear friend Rosa was my cool neighbor about ten years older. She had seen a lot of the world and her share of trauma. She possessed grit and determination. Her slender, tall, striking form and deep voice made her alluring to others. We instantly became friends even though I was in my first career right out of college and thought I knew so much. Rosa had a relaxed, laid-back style while I was a bundle of smiles and energy all day long. In dog terms, think of an Elkhound hanging out with a jumping Red Spaniel puppy. What Rosa saw in me was baffling since she was sophisticated and worldly. Well, one night, Rosa invited me over for a dinner party to meet Saundra, her longtime closest friend, who was coming into town. Ironically, I spent time planning what to bring to be a good guest, yet it never dawned on me to prepare how to behave as a good dinner guest. Instead, that night was a disaster because I failed to read all the other social clues floating in the room.

Seeing Rosa and Saundra laughing made me feel awkward. I naively had not expected she had another best friend. They were finishing each other's jokes and stories and talking about shared memories. I felt lost in the room and clueless about how to behave, so I would fit in. I couldn't even name what emotions I felt. It wasn't their fault. They did everything correct to include me in the fun evening. Yet, I still felt like an outsider.

Insecurity and jealousy bubbled up. Those unfamiliar emotions made me react entirely polar to my usual self. Unfortunately, strong feelings can turn nervous energy into something bizarre, and it did. It made me babble. That insecurity caused me to ramble on all about myself and monopolized the conversations without listening to Rosa or befriending Saundra. Why? Because it was much easier to talk about something I knew, me.

Here's the worst part of the tale. I thought the night went well. I believed I was a good guest at the dinner party and clueless that I acted like a jerk. Rosa had invited me over to meet her other best friend, and my conduct should have been inclusive for us all to become friends, not isolated and braggadocious. It was not a time for me to talk constantly about myself, but a time to be curious about the guest coming into town. I should have asked Saundra questions and focused attention on her arrival to see her best friend. Before arriving, I should have spent some time considering what conversations might be interesting or actions might be helpful. Had I done so, I would have been prepared with a backup plan and not allowed my emotions to make me the fool. That evening should have been a time for them to celebrate a reunion, with maybe a small contribution from me. I could have learned more about Rosa if I'd been aware and paid attention. I was a lot like Ray (in our earlier story), who wasn't interested in anyone else and became a bore to others.

Awareness Check Time – Would I Be Able to Recover?
How did I find out I blew it? That is the good news. I was educated and, thankfully, made aware of my mistakes. After that evening, I didn't see or hear from Rosa, even after leaving a message thanking her for dinner. She purposely waited a week then asked to see me for coffee. I could feel something was off but would never have guessed in a million years how I had caused her such grief. I was totally clueless!

Rosa said she had something to talk over with me and hoped I could simply listen. I was shocked when she shared that she and Saundra were disappointed with how the evening turned out. It was all my fault. Wow! At first, I felt offended, thinking, "How could Rosa be unaware that I was lost and confused?" I gulped and took a deep breath, giving my brain some oxygen. Then, once I visualized how the evening went and the emotions I felt, it made me sad to realize she was right. It was a painful lesson.

I felt terrible knowing Rosa was disappointed by her failed efforts to mix her local best friend and her longtime best friend. I then realized how brave Rosa had been to communicate her feelings with me candidly. Rosa had a choice on what to do with our friendship. She cared enough that she chose to approach me and talk about the problem. She must have believed I could change. Rosa decided to see if I could be a better friend in the future. If she had not done that, our friendship would have died that night. I, too, had a choice to make. I chose to listen and not play the victim, feeling insulted and reprimanded. I decided to learn from the specific feedback provided by one of my best friends. I learned from her expectations of how a true friend should behave.

Rosa must have developed her list of qualities and traits of how a true friend should act, and I was held to those standards. This is an excellent example of why knowing what you expect in others, and wanting in a true friend, will identify someone who misses the mark. If only we could go back in time. Right? To this day, I remember when I blew it at that dinner and consciously remind myself not to monopolize conversations or events when the day is about someone else. Fortunately, Rosa reflected on that terrible dinner party, took time to regain her composure, and realized my behavior was temporary and fixable. She allowed me to demonstrate I would not repeat being insensitive and overbearing when mixing with her inner circle. She gave me space and grace to evolve into a true friend worthy of her time and devotion.

If you are faced with a similar situation, remember you have a choice. Depending on which side of the conversation you are on, it is up to you to take action. If nothing is done, that most likely will kill a friendship. If the friendship is of great value, the investment of your time and energy to fix the issue is probably going to make sense over time. Once again, always remember, we have choices to make. Doing nothing (to communicate or improve our relationships) results in getting nothing.

Friendships with Expiration Dates

Not all stories end well, like with Rosa and me. Over the past chapters, we briefly touched on the possibility a friendship might not always last. Some friendships have *invisible* expiration dates. Not all do, but sad endings are normal in life. What are some red flags that a friendship may no longer be healthy (using the above exercise)?

Red Flag Test - Your Friendships May Need Reflection:

- You make a date and usually, they cancel at the last minute.
- You rearranged your plans to fit their busy schedule, and they forget your date again.
- You share a heartfelt issue and without pause, they direct the conversation back to them.
- You repeatedly wish they could listen when you "speak your truth."
- You've become angry or disappointed they ignored something you shared and felt was important.
- When you are suffering, they fail to notice, listen, or try to understand.
- Your friend does not celebrate your wins or milestones.
- You feel they compete with you. Whatever you share, they want to outshine.
- Your confidence and trust shared were broken by something they did or said.
- You leave repeatedly feeling drained or uncertain after spending time together.
- All their conversations are about their world, problems, goals, plans, and emotions.
- They forget an important date or tradition shared in your friendship.

- When you mention they forgot an important date for you, they say they had remembered and then offer no apologies or remorse for being absent-minded and not reaching out.
- You feel this behavior was odd for a close friend, yet that's how they've always acted.

Time for Some Friendship Maintenance?

Now, pause a moment and consider who you make time for in your busy life. Did those people pass the red flag test above, or did many of those behaviors describe certain friends? Downsizing (pruning the garden) the number of friends we interact with may be in our best interests. Yet, it can feel mean-spirited even to think about it. So instead of addressing problems, we tolerate bad behavior because it wasn't quite egregious enough, or we weren't ready to walk away from that friendship yet. Even though they became a friend no longer worthy of true friendship, we feel compelled by loyalty to hang in there, hoping they will improve. Isn't that like putting sour milk back in the refrigerator, thinking it will taste better another day?

Now that you've increased your awareness and know what qualities you most desire in others, keep your eyes open and observe. Look for red-flag actions like the ones described above. You can add to or develop your own red flags list. Use it to build your awareness of a friendship on the decline or needing attention. It's like deciding you want to buy a specific car in a particular color. Once sensitive to seeing that specific car, the interstate shows it to you because you paid attention. That happens because we stimulate a part of the brain that alerts us to specific details. Once you focus on actions that are not how true friends behave, you will notice if a pattern exists in their behavior.

Past performance is the best indicator of future performance, but even the best of us have bad days or months. If their behavior is temporarily "glitched" and you can reasonably expect them to correct it, give them a chance to do so. However, if there is a seasoned pattern, be honest with yourself. That's when you must decide if they are changeable and worthy of having a candid discussion, like Rosa did with me.

When You Are the One Left Behind and Don't Know Why – The Death of a Friendship

Often, the hardest part about being the friend abandoned is that you were not aware it was coming. It may have happened already, and you completely missed it. It is almost impossible to fathom that they just don't feel the same way about you anymore. Why? Because you still care for that friend. It's a super hard truth to admit because we missed the signs. It may have begun with a friend drifting away, and you assume it is because you are both so busy. You text or talk about trying to set up dates (see red flags section above), but the responses never come, or the dates never happen.

TRUTH BOMB:

When someone says they will TRY to see you or TRY to call you later, that means they have little or no intention of doing so. Try is a wasted word, and I highly recommend you remove it from your vocabulary. It is not a commitment, nor is it a prediction of any action that will happen. For example, we try to lose weight, try not to engage in that bad habit again, try to remember people's names. Those are all prevarications. If someone plans to see you or call you, they say, "I want to set up a time, how about next Saturday at 2:00 p.m." Or "I will call you on the ride home tonight to catch up. Let's get something confirmed for sure to meet up." That is how true friends talk, followed by what they do. They don't say, "I will try to call you when I am back in town in June." Don't hold your breath waiting for that call.

The second sign of a friendship fading is usually missed too and is one of the red flags covered above. They set up a date with you and forget, or worse than that; they cancel at the last moment. I missed many signs that one of my longtime friends was fading away. She struggled to raise her daughter, manage a household with her demanding career, and handle her mom's relocation. I saw her life as chaotic and knew we'd catch up in the future. I didn't realize she no longer valued our friendship. I was no longer a priority in her life. We had shared so much over the years and had become such trusted friends that I assumed we would be friends for life. I naively believed that if you were my dear friend, we would grow old together too. I missed seeing the "death of a friendship" signs. I missed seeing she had an invisible friendship expiration date. Since her life was in constant chaos, I would rearrange my busy work calendar to align with hers, and she'd either forget or cancel at the last minute. On two occasions, I rescheduled clients, which cost me time and money. This went on for eight months. Clearly, this indicated our meetup was not a priority, or perhaps something significant had happened in her world. I kept making excuses.

Since I couldn't reach her in-person, I thought hearing my voice and tone would be reassuring. Remember we talked about how vocal communication is 38% effective because they can listen to your tone. So, I phoned and left a voicemail. "Hey there, are you alright? We've set up several dates to catch up, and you've had to cancel at the last minute. I miss you and hope all is ok in your world. If you need anything, I am here to help, or if I've missed something that has happened between us, please let me know—sending my love and hugs. Take care."
A total soul shocker happened! The next day, I received her text. I opened it thinking it would be her update about what's been going on. Instead, I had to sit down while reading her unbelievable words. My heart fell on the floor, and I could not breathe. She texted to say, *"I am alright, just busy. I have always loved being your friend and appreciating what we shared over the years. You haven't done anything. Our lives are just different now, so it doesn't make sense to be friends."*

Oh, my goodness! I was speechless and sat there, stunned. Did she end our 18-year friendship with a text? Seriously. That's how she decided to communicate with someone who had been her best friend? Not even a phone call. It felt like the TV Show episode when the lead's (Carrie) boyfriend leaves her a sticky Post-it note on the bathroom mirror, saying, "I'm sorry this isn't working for me any longer." No explanation or energy, just a post-it note. Carrie was befuddled and humiliated. That was all the thought he had given to her.

When it's Time to Say Goodbye – The Death of Your Friendship

As you can see, deciding to end a friendship is complicated and must be done with great care. Breaking up with someone you've shared friendship with over the years deserves your personal touch to honor the person. Just because you find yourself ready to move on doesn't mean you should be indifferent about how it is handled. Plan how to communicate your feelings to the person you once regarded as your friend. Share your updated feelings gently to let them know you are moving in a different circle now. Do not send them a text or a social media message or have it come from a third party. Your goal is to exit the relationship on good terms and not hurt the other person's feelings. If your friendship is now not valued as much, that is alright. Things change, and people evolve. In the long run, it is far better to end a friendship than continue one that makes no sense or is only one-sided. You have to be truthful with yourself while at the same time remember there is another person who will be affected by you walking away. Of course, don't underestimate how much they care for you and plan for that. If you mean a great deal in their lives, they will go through a grieving process because it is a loss. Remember, they have not had time to adjust to you no longer being in their lives. They may have been more invested in the friendship than you from the very beginning. Take the high road and don't leave them not understanding why you've peeled off in their life. They probably missed what you thought were crystal clear signs because they thought you had been too busy and would resurface later—the mistake I made. Instead, you suddenly appear, announcing your friendship status is no longer the same. See how confusing that can be to your friend? Hold in your heart that you cared about them in the past when you now say it's over.

If you are sure it is time to end a friendship, and not due to some unforgivable act, find a time to talk openly with your friend. If you are more comfortable using Facetime or the phone, that is fine. Your goal is to exit while allowing your friend to understand that nothing they have purposefully done drove you away. Perhaps your interests or values have changed over the years, and you now need something different. For example, when I left the corporate world, I no longer wanted to hear about the horrible work conditions we endured. To keep some friendships, I insisted we would omit such stories from our conversations and focus on how to be friends outside of the workplace. Some friends could adjust; others could not. Another example is when friends are originally drawn together as drinking-party buddies and then go on having families. They must find shared interests outside the bar scene. Otherwise, the friendships fade away.

The Art of Letting Go – Have the Courage to Say Farewell

Be gracious and thoughtful enough to pause and honor your shared past with this person. You've decided you need to move forward reshaping your future friendships, yet it can be a shocker for your friend. It's easier to let go of an old friend when it coincides with a physical relocation to another city. Everyone anticipates the possibility that distance will fade bonds once shared. However, if it is not a relocation that fades your friendship, please share the changes you feel are happening in your world or theirs, making your friendship no longer a strong fit. Approach that conversation from the point of love and be aware they need time to absorb how things will change.

I don't recommend discussing your feelings regarding a mutual friend in your circle before you have your private chat. Your friend deserves to hear from you how you are feeling. It is incredibly painful and unfair to your friend to learn second-hand why you no longer want to be part of their world. Besides, others don't typically share what you said word-for-word. It ends up a distorted version that can be harsh, cruel, or at the very least inaccurate. That makes it seem more like gossip. Those actions also hurt you in the future because you become less attractive to potential true friends who may be watching. Remember that we discussed in earlier chapters how we are all being observed? How you handle separating yourself from others determines if you are viewed as recklessly abandoning former friendships or being loyal to your inner circle.

Times Change – We Have Nothing in Common – They Don't Feel the Same About You

Just as I had to request my former co-worker friends stop talking about work, there can be times when a relationship has greatly changed, and we are no longer friends. Temporary friendships can start as friends of convenience forced together by an activity (soccer parents), or a cause (volunteer), or an environment (workplace). Such a forced friendship happened to my friend, April. She worked with her boss, Cassie, for decades and finally could financially resign. They had a huge farewell party, and she thought she'd never see those people again. Yet her ex-boss continued to call, asking her to go out just like they had always done. At first, April would make excuses. Eventually, they met for lunch, and April kept thinking the whole event seemed bizarre. She agreed to lunch, hoping to find a common interest, non-work related, that would support a friendship. Instead, it became apparent all they ever had in common was work.

April did not feel the same connection Cassie did. April said to me, "I've seen myself as an employee, not as a friend!" In her mind, for over ten years, April never allowed the two relationships to mingle. Sadly, her ex-boss misinterpreted their connection as a deep friendship and grieved not seeing April in her daily life anymore. Her ex-boss naively thought they'd continue seeing each other. April gently let her ex-boss know it was great to catch up, and their time together was wonderful, yet she was now in a different world. It was a soft-closure approach to remove herself from more lunch invites. April still sends a friendly card to her ex-boss on special occasions. However, she no longer feels compelled to accept lunch invitations.

My "No, He Didn't!" Story - Liar! Liar! Pants on Fire – Death of a Couples Friendship

In college, my world opened up to an influx of new types of people. I believed then, as now, we are supposed to learn something from everyone. I later found that what you learn can be shocking and brutal to accept, but the truth is the truth, even if it is bad about a friend.

My boyfriend became friends with a busy entrepreneur couple who seemed to have it all. Cassandra was beautiful, vibrant, and witty, with a wild drive to succeed. She was a beauty and quite memorable when she locked eyes with you. Cane, her husband, was a bland and well-respected businessman with a big smile and an engaging, nurturing spirit. They made a perfect couple with their creative entrepreneurial talents.

One night they proclaimed their invention was almost finished and asked, "Would you like to see it after dinner?" I was awestruck again. Who were these people? How could they think and talk so differently than everyone I had known? All my neighbors and friends either worked for a company or the government. I loved seeing Cassandra promoting products on TV. I'd sit there, nodding, proudly saying, "Those are my friends." It excited me to witness their success. My interest continued to grow, and I wondered what their next big enterprise would be over the next two years of cookouts and big dreams. I loved helping them with the vision and hammering out ideas on building the businesses and marketplace. They were a huge hit—a smart couple on their way to make millions because they worked hard with a great plan. Their places opened, and one by one, each became a huge success. Our friendships felt like a magical blessing. Being the youngest in the group, I watched and always learned from them.

Well, my social education wasn't complete. I was about to learn something I never expected in a million years. Behind the calm, nurturing demeanor of Cassandra's husband lurked a stranger. I had no clue or indication of what truth bomb was heading our way. One night at our usual dinner party, Cassandra seemed withdrawn and sad. She shared her turmoil over an accusation made by an employee against her husband, Cane. Our first reaction was outrage. This complaint must have come from an angry rival with a misplaced temper, and justice would prevail for our friend. My only question to my friend was, "Did you do what they are saying?"

Without any delay, Cane looked me in my eyes, and replied, "No." We left that night feeling a pit in our stomachs. What would happen to the super couple who had it all?

The months passed slowly, and we all held our breaths. We still believed this was a colossal mistake, and our dear friend would be acquitted. My heart ached for Cassandra and her family. How mortifying this all must be. I could not imagine her mix of emotions. Then a newspaper landed on my doorstep, revealing the truth with a headline, reading the words that I can never erase from my memory—Local Business Leader Pleads Guilty to Drug Dealing. As I read court-recorded comments, a cold sweat broke out, and I ran to throw up. How could this be? His betrayal of everyone. He looked me in my eyes and professed his innocence. I believed his load of bull. My heart was outraged and pounding, for Cassandra's sake, my dear friend. She deserved so much better in a man. Everything they built was falling like a house of cards.

We tried to help Cassandra, but she was not ready to connect. The embarrassment and emotional roller coaster were too real. We watched from the sidelines as their next year(s) were spent with lawsuits, financial trauma, counseling therapy, and just struggling to survive. Their marriage collapsed. It continued to baffle us. It was like discovering Jekyll and Hyde in your inner circle.

Betrayal is a weird act to deal with in a friendship or any relationship. It comes in many forms. Betrayal is super sneaky because it defies our ability to apply the needed logic by hijacking our minds with an overload of heartfelt emotions. After all, we do not want to believe our friends are capable of terrible deeds. Therefore, it cannot be true.

Ten years later, when I ran into Cassandra standing in a to-go line. She was glad to see me and vice versa. Her zeal and beauty were less bright. The years had taken a toll. I still adored her yet realized our friendship could never be as it was. She had remarried, and they had two wonderful children. I shared how I wished her much happiness because she deserved it in life. She was a wonderful person. I never mentioned the past trauma. I didn't want to make her hurt again, yet I'm still not sure ignoring the elephant in the room was the right thing to do.

TRUTH BOMB:

If that friendship were today, I would have made the bold move to tell Cassandra how much I loved our friendship and continued to pray for her healing. Additionally, I would have asked for her new mailing address to send a card or flowers for everything she'd taught me years ago. Her friendship with me was something I did not intentionally wish to end. Cassandra, I hope God and His blessings have followed you.

When Faced with a Call to Action

Just because someone is a jerk or creep in actions unrelated to you does not mean they were not your real friend. Humans are flawed by nature. However, it does not mean you have to continue being someone's friend if they violate what you consider a core value, moral, trust. So when faced with a betrayal of character by a friend, weigh their conduct carefully against your qualities, traits, and character standards. If you decide it's time to walk away, ensure you communicate your best regards to any collateral people, like Cassandra. Those collateral people need support while their world crumbles.

How to Evaluate a "No, You Didn't!" Moment

The following questions are to be used when faced with a situation when a friend's behavior was disappointing or outraged you. Your answers can help you determine if that person needs to exit your circle. In reality, you could have assumed an innocent person to be guilty or a guilty person to be innocent. For the sake of these reflection questions below, we believe the friend to have behaved poorly, but you could ask it the other way if you want to analyze it deeper.

 PONDERING PAUSE:

- Has someone in your inner or work circle been rumored to have done something terribly wrong?
- How did you react?
- When you learned the truth, do you wish you had initially reacted the same or differently?

Understanding The Death of a Friendship

With every true friendship, there is always the possibility it will not stand the test of time. We've explored many reasons why someone chooses to stop being a friend and how best to handle the breakup instead of drifting away. We've discussed how friendships end or evolve in response to significant change: new work, a new circle of friends, relocations, different values, drama, substance abuse, and so on. Also, not everyone equally values each friend the same on an emotional level. The death of a friendship is a complicated topic to address because, in some cases, it needs to end, like my story of Cane the predator. Act honorably in ways you will be proud of yourself when you reflect at the end of the day. Breaking up with a friend, left behind, or ignored causes heartache, especially in women. Some of us are too embarrassed to admit we handled a situation poorly in the past with a friend, resulting in the friendship's death. We discussed the worst (text and post-it-note) ways to end a friendship, and the best (transparent loving conversation). I'm sure you agree by now; ending a relationship is an acquired skill. Even if you have made mistakes in the past, you can still do better in the future. Why? Because you now have some training to help.

Hopefully, you've gained an insight into your inner circle from completing the exercises and pondering pauses provided. Your goal is to build up your skills to measure your inner circle against the qualities and traits desired more in friends. Throughout life, it is best to analyze and determine if everyone is still a good fit. As we've learned, naming aloud our genuine emotions and how we feel after we spend time together is a truth worth finding. If you start to decide a person is no longer a good fit in your world, you can apply your new skills to exit a friendship gracefully, with awareness, and kindness. It's always best if you can look back and be proud of your actions. Now, let's talk about those unexpected friendships that happen in life called situational friendships. These types of people surround us every day. It is your decision and actions taken that affect how those situational related relationships evolve. As we move on in our next chapter, we will explore how they can or cannot be your potential friends.

CHAPTER 9
SITUATIONAL AND EVOLVING FRIENDSHIPS

We've explored how gaining a variety of friendships can expand your mind and make life more enjoyable. Hopefully, you are now increasing your awareness to find potential friends with varied backgrounds and interests. Additional times where you should be more aware of the opportunity to collect friends are situations based on proximity and circumstance. I call these partial choices. You choose where to work, but you cannot select the other employees. You decide where to live, but cannot choose the neighbors, and so on.

During the busiest times in your life, you can easily overlook the opportunity to embrace people you see daily as potential friends. Though you see them frequently, you always see them the same way. For example, this happens in family settings where adult siblings cannot stop viewing each other as mere siblings. Or the coworker who is only seen as a "work friend." Or the couple who live three houses down is "just neighbors." These classifications are mental blocks preventing relationships from evolving. Examples of limiting mindsets are things like, "I have enough friends" or "that is not my type of friend." If you are not willing to pursue a possible connection, you lose an opportunity to *Collect a True Friend*.

Situational relationships also arise from places we frequent. We need to use our discernment skills when situations introduce people into our lives. Some of them may be good choices for our inner circle, and others should be kept at a distance. You may know their name, their face, and you have a basic relationship based on a situation. For example, like the partying crowd who frequented a bar starts learning about each other's names or football stadiums with season tickets. The question to ask is, "Do I select this person to be elevated to a higher level?" Should I transition that person to a friend?

Some potential friendships quicken from having a high level of natural trust established with others at the location. A situational setting like sports, church, charities, school, or community projects brings people together for a reason. Let's explore the various types of situations that may present friendship opportunities. As you roll through these types of situations, consider who you know today that fits into each category. Write their name down to compare it against your desired qualities list created in Chapter 3. You may discover a few *unkindled* friendships to pursue.

Coworkers

Employment is a situation where we are pushed together and forced to act cordially and thoughtfully with a wide variety of people. Workplaces will offer you a high volume of people to meet and observe. Many of my best long-term friendships started in the workplace. Even though we moved on to other careers, we remained friends. When nurtured, these connections can become your greatest assets. How so? The hours of collaboration spent accomplishing projects build an excellent foundation for trust first then friendship. If you can work successfully together, trust has already been demonstrated by relying on one another and delivering promises. When you learn how someone thinks and acts, a relationship will develop naturally. You may realize the person is a good fit in your life, or you may form an unfavorable opinion. Why do so many of our business contacts and coworkers keep a distance? From my experience, this is an old-fashioned mindset based on generations of training that there is a recognized hierarchy in business, plus, an antiquated concern for fraternization. I consider that to be a stale view.

We should treat coworkers at all levels with respect because of their position, but remember, they are people who might make good friends. The mechanic with dirty hands and tools is as likely to be a great friend as is the senior leader in coat and tie. If coworkers and business contacts could treat each other more like potential friends, workdays could feel more comfortable with less strife. Remember to use your Qualities List made in Chapter 4 to help identify ideal friends in a workplace.

 PONDERING PAUSE:

Notice how people act at an event or in the business-setting and do this reflection.

- Does a person working or meeting near me possess the traits and qualities I identified as desirable?
- Do I find them appealing as a potential friend?
- Do they talk about activities that fascinate me?
- Do I lean in to hear them talk about their weekend and family?
- Are their actions aligned with how I treat others?
- Could I commit to being open to knowing them better as a person and not see just their title or what they do at work?
- Would I consider inviting that person to something casual and fun in the future?

Be approachable and act professionally with everyone, including those visiting vendors and colleagues at your workplace. If others might not understand your friendship with a coworker or outsider, then be discreet. Don't stop pursuing ideal friendships with someone based solely on what others might think. They may not be interested in gaining more quality friendships like you are committed to now. Some of my best friends started as professional acquaintances. We worked in distinct functions and separated our business responsibilities from our friendship. The lesson here is to embrace opportunities for friendships with those you meet and see frequently. For example, the people you are tasked to work with on a team or project might be like-minded potential friends. You may leave a job in the future and take away with you those true friends collected along the way. It is your choice. Your actions determine if you make friends in workplace or business-related situations.

TIP:

- If you are in an office or business setting, adjust your mindset that friendships are a possible bonus.
- Ignore titles and see the person in front of you for their qualities.
- Train yourself to be more aware of anyone who shares the same values and traits and tactfully explore that connection.

TRUTH BOMB:

New research shows that workers who make friends at work are happier and more productive, which increases employee retention. Therefore, a friendship-friendly environment is beneficial to both the employer and employee.

Neighbors

Being a good neighbor seems to be a foreign concept for many people. Friendship opportunities surround us every day, yet many fail to befriend those near home. It wasn't that way a hundred years ago. Technology and mobility have made us less dependent on neighboring families to thrive and trade. Today, someone buys or rents a place and is surprised when their neighbors stop by to welcome them to the neighborhood. Sadly, I have heard people comment they believed it felt intrusive when others welcomed them to the neighborhood. Only later did they realize they were the ones not open enough to inviting neighborly kindness. They were unaccustomed to a good Samaritan living near them.

Depending on how a person was raised, some are simply unfamiliar with receiving a warm gesture of greeting. Likewise, they fail to realize it is good manners to speak with their neighbors and welcome them to the community. The Bible tells us to "love thy neighbor." Those are not just words. It is a way of life. Everyone should strive to put that philosophy into action. Why? Because community is a vital part of everyone's existence. When a community thrives, everyone benefits. Being neighborly is more than just flashing a smile that promotes connection. Being consistent and positive is what makes you a good neighbor. Those qualities also attract more principled people into your world. Not everyone in your neighborhood will qualify to be part of your inner circle. That is alright. Just keep using your awareness and discernment skills to isolate any that misbehave from getting closer. The good news is the majority living near you are usually great people. You already have one positive thing in common. They chose that exact location to reside for many of the reasons your family did.

The surprising part is neighbors can be an excellent source of long-term true friendships. Becoming a great neighbor and adored in the community will make it much easier for others to like and trust you. This is especially true when you are the new neighbor. Believe me. I remember being the *Little Viking Girl* moving into another new city and community. My mom would bake something and take it to our adjacent houses. She did this to make an excellent first impression. That simple act helped broadcast us as kind people and made others more receptive to strangers. When an existing neighbor shares kind comments regarding newcomers, doors open, and friendship opportunities increase, when someone of influence acts inclusive and welcoming in their community or neighborhood, others who trust them will follow.

What are the ways you can gain your neighbors' favor? Even if you've lived there for a while, you can still gain others' trust if you *slowly* begin to make these gestures of kindness. Here are a few ways to start.
- Smile and say hello to someone walking past your home.
- Wave to those running by or walking their dog.
- Speak to the mailman.
- Wave or nod at those driving or biking past.
- Offer to volunteer in your homeowner's association. (Pick an easy project for your schedule.)

- Pay attention and assist a neighbor if you see a need. It could be something as small as bringing in their trash can or as big as showing up with a chainsaw to take down a tree. Function within your capabilities, of course.
- Offer to host the neighbor's garden or cleanup club.
- Offer to invite a food truck into your neighborhood to socialize with the neighbors.

TRUTH BOMB:

Research shows that one of the most significant factors in living a long, healthy life is a sense of community. Living in a place where you feel comfortable and belong to the area increases longevity. That's what nurturing friendships in your neighborhood can do for your health and well-being as well as theirs.

We Became Friends for Our Kid's Sake

Raising three daughters meant constant exposure to the parents of our kids' friends. Many of those became longtime friends that, even today, we cherish. Other parents would never have been chosen as our friends. These are situational relationships. You are forced together by a shared activity. In this case, we were all united in the raising of our children. We helped each other by carpooling and supervising activities. In such situational settings, you do not need to become close friends with the parents merely because your kids became best friends. Especially if their values or priorities misalign instead, it is necessary to be genuine and friendly for your kid's sake. It helps to stay aware of the common reason why you are connected. Friendships will either continue or end as the children move in different directions.

Raising our three daughters made us spend endless hours camping and standing on soccer fields with hundreds of parents. Occasionally, there would be a jerk parent with poor values. They were clueless to other parents cringing in disbelief. For example, the stressed-out lawyer parent ran onto our kid's soccer field in mid-game to cuss out the referee. When the referee told this outraged parent to exit the area, he returned to our sidelines and tossed his folding chair into our crowd. WOW! Now that's a guy we instantly decided to never let near our inner circle. Sadly, he felt he was right. After all, he was defending the team from a wrong referee call. Nope! Significant issues were going on in his life that made him unacceptable to befriend.

Then there is another type of annoying parent you reluctantly befriend, even when you think a relationship could become trouble. She's the one that runs up to you and rambles on and on about her "business opportunity." You explain you are not interested in the product line she sells. Then she asks you to have a home party to "help her out." She tugs on you emotionally, saying, "Our kids are best friends." You want to be nice, so you buy something as a gesture of kindness to support her business. Yet, that is not enough. It quickly rolls like a snowball into an avalanche. Now she thinks it's an opening to recruit you for her sales team. Have you experienced that person? These are what I call "situationally forced temporary friendships." They happen when you are coerced into accepting someone in your world due to proximity. In this circumstance, continue to stay friendly and declarative in your boundaries. They will move onto another target person soon enough.

Another excellent example of a situational relationship happens when you volunteer on a school project, and a parent requests a favor prematurely. When we collectively work on a project or community goal, people can unknowingly overstep their familiarity. In this circumstance, it is best to let the person know you've just joined the group, and perhaps later you'd be open to discuss their request.

TRUTH BOMB:

Collaborating on a community event does not instantly convert strangers into friends. Trust happens after we know, watch, and begin to like someone.

We've discussed that everyone watches each other before inviting any form of friendship. Time spent together will usually build trust, since we can observe their values and interactions. We've established that being mutually connected through your child's best friend will not instantly create trust. It is more of a place to start. So, how can we gain others confidence and trust in these situational relationships? There are three ingredients: show acts of kindness, keep your promises, and be consistently favorable in your disposition. Those key factors will decide who will know, like, and trust.

TIP:

Not everyone needs to become your friend just because you are regularly forced together. If the parents are less than ideal, that should not block the kids from forming a solid friendship. When our children befriend each other, it is our duty to role-model excellent friendship qualities. Including teaching them awareness and discernment skills to help them identify those worthy of being in their inner circle.

FRIENDSHIPS THAT COULD EVOLVE

Transitioning Adult Siblings to Friends

"All I am asking them to do is treat me with mutual respect! If my siblings truly want to fix our relationships, this time, we will have some boundaries. I am not that same little kid they led around for years. I get it; they are my big brother and big sister, but I am not going to let them bully me anymore. If they genuinely want me back in the family's life, they will stop expecting an apology every time they get angry about something. I've apologized my whole life to keep peace in our family. It is time they treat me as an equal like they do non-family members." Does that dialogue sound familiar? This situational relationship happens when a person refuses to transition into a relationship with someone younger.

Relationships can fail to evolve among siblings when their initial pecking order anchors family roles for a lifetime. Families are notorious for pigeon-holing a member and not recognizing that a member has developed. Not realizing how another person has matured can create an unhealthy relationship. When siblings refuse to acknowledge each other as adults, they can never become friends.

How can siblings transition from one type of relationship to become friends? If you were the oldest, it probably felt easier to be in charge. Now your advice may not be requested as much, even when you know the magical answer they need. They don't want to hear what you have to say right now. Consequently, your siblings' behaviors can seem mind-boggling. This happens when others choose not to accept the relative as a grown version. They want them to behave the same as when they lived together.

This lack of acknowledging another's status is also a typical situation that occurs between parents and children. For example, when someone is senior in age or title, they expect others to treat them in a revered status. Opportunities for a different kind of relationship, however, can happen. To allow the relationship to evolve, each must update perceptions and behaviors towards the other person. Beautiful friendships can develop from situational relationships when both are willing to update their roles. Yet, this can be a big challenge for many because change can be frightening. It can make them feel misunderstood, underappreciated, or even insecure. Their identity roles are being redefined. Occasionally, anger rears its ugly head as a dominant emotion and confuses everyone.

What I recently learned about anger is that it is rooted in fear. If we can return to our senses and examine anger more closely, we can discover the cause. Why would anger bubble up when people who have known each other their whole lives need to be able to effectively communicate? Perhaps it is a fear of abandonment? Fear of loss? Fear of failing? Fear they will not see each other anymore?

That is why it is necessary to understand the reason behind the sibling's reluctance to act differently and transition into their relationship. For example, they might be afraid that if they behave with less control in the family dynamics, others won't need or revere them as much. Identifying obstacles to change in situational relationships allows you the time to address the potential for creating any friendship.

Siblings must understand that their brothers and sisters grow into adults. Their siblings have become educated, moved on, and have full lives. To become friends, they must accept their siblings as "social equals." The relationships that can evolve are the ones that accept new boundaries. Those might be, for example, having less frequent talks or agreeing to omit specific conversation topics. It can feel challenging for siblings at the top of the pecking order when they think their status is being diminished. They may not even understand why they feel insecure. Siblings who can evolve into true friends (as adults) are the ones who love each other enough to acknowledge and accept each other as they are today. They do not enforce their antiquated role as "kid sister" or "big brother" in how they communicate or interact. It is possible to make that happen. When I mingle among siblings who act more like friends than family members, I stand in awe. It is a beautiful thing seeing brothers and sisters who are also loving and supportive friends enjoying spending time together.

Transitioning from Parent to Friend

It is hard for me to admit this following belief about parenting. I believe it is much easier to raise a child than build a healthy new relationship with them as adults. When they are children, they follow their leader (parent) as the authority figure. For their safety and well-being, we instruct them on what to do and not to do. Most of the time, they follow our instructions. Then, over time, their willingness to receive helpful direction fades. When people comment on how frustrating it is to raise teenagers and why they act that way, I tell them it is nature's plan. When they are ready to leave, you are ready to let them go.

When kids become adults, they want to be seen as social equals, and likewise, be asked for their advice, like siblings do when they grow up. That transition cannot happen if we continue to treat them like children. No longer do they need reminders on daily to-dos from a parent. They especially hate being overloaded with too many questions. Yet, if a parent cannot make that transition, a friendship connection can never be allowed to grow. Sadly, not everyone can transition from being a hands-on parent to the friendship level. Some find it overly exhausting and drift away. However, if you are a parent, imagine yourself much older and wouldn't you want to visualize yourself talking and laughing with your son or daughter like they were a friend?

When raising children, you might have proclaimed, "I am not your friend. I am your parent." Young children must initially accept you in that role, but that changes as the child becomes a teenager and more determined to challenge authority. Even though you are still biologically their parent, they are "social equals," and you must accept that your position has changed. Give them the same respect you would any adult and try genuinely to relate to their world. It would help if you continued to offer advice, but as any friend would, since you no longer have the social authority to impose your rules on them. That is a significant distinction. The good news is you have some built-in advantages. Your children already know you well, realize you have their best interest at heart, and trust you. You are not starting from scratch to form a friendship. So how can great friendships develop and evolve between a parent and child when all known rules of parent engagement change?

Here are some helpful cues that your parent – child relationship is in a transition phase. If this applies to you, please take some time to consider if you need to transition from parenting mode into a friendship. The earlier you become aware of this change, the more time you will have to develop a friendship.

- Mannerisms you used before are not received well now.
- Each side gets confused or upset during conversations.
- They rebel and pull away in frustration on established old rules and behaviors.
- Withdrawal happens. Someone is shocked.
- They no longer seek or depend on parental advice.
- They want to be treated as equals and more like friends.
- The parental role feels exhausting.
- The son or daughter keeps withdrawing from interactions.

 TIP:

Hear this fact loud and clear. To keep someone you value in your life, you must adjust how you act. You cannot change them. However, you have the ability to change yourself if you decide it is a priority. Here is the truth bomb. If you do not update your relationship mannerisms, you face the possibility they will exit your life. You have a choice.

If you are willing to transition from a hands-on (helicopter) parent to a trusted friend, be aware that is a significant step. It requires rebuilding what you have into a situational friendship. All the strategies and rules on friendship building discussed previously apply. Many things have to be set into motion to create a friendship out of an original parent – child relationship.

- Become aware change is coming.
- Accept that the old rules don't work anymore. What worked in the past needs an overhaul.
- Encourage a mutual acceptance of the need for change.
- Talk calmly to one another about what each would like their relationship to be.
- Identify specific areas which irritate one another. (Talk kindly and do not start an argument.)
- Name the trigger-moments and topics that seem to flare emotions.
- List the good things about your current relationship. For example, your offer to check on their dogs if they work late. You will always pick up their phone calls.
- Identify key mistakes to avoid. For example, you are overly curious in your questioning.
- Do a progress check.

Mother – Daughter Relationship

One of the most challenging relationships to transition is the mother – daughter connection. When a daughter grows up, friendship is precisely what she needs from a mother. She no longer needs daily instruction. Grown daughters crave being seen as capable of making good decisions. This is challenging for a devoted parent whose entire focus was on her daughter's well-being, and now she must engage less. As we've discussed, creating a friendship starts with the ability to spot when a transition is happening. There is always a choice. You can choose to ignore the transition, but it is going to happen, anyway. It does not mean the emotional attachment ends. It means your relationship cannot survive within the same structure. A better choice is to engage with the daughter to manage the change actively. Timing is crucial. Delay can result in missed opportunities and bring about an unfavorable result.

If a mom believes that her grown child always needs to listen and follow, because she is (supposedly) wiser, the mother – daughter relationship stagnates. Everyone must grow at their own pace, whether in families, friendships, or work. This fact exists in all forms of friendship. You may be the wiser one right now on a specific subject, yet as others gain experience, they can surpass your expertise. That doesn't mean your knowledge is no longer of value. It means that, as in all friendships, shared information is best when offered at appropriate times and in small doses. The last two generations grew up using Google and YouTube to learn anything at a glance. Asking elders for information was not their norm. Granted, there are still some traditional things we need to share with the younger generation personally—wisdom on childbirth, marriage, customs, power of faith, financial guidance, and more.

TRUTH BOMB:

Over the last 100 years, the world changed more quickly than ever before because of communications technology. It was no longer the case where older generations taught technology to the younger generations. Mothers should listen more to their daughters because they are skilled in technology and shortcuts to make our lives easier and happier. They bring a different kind of wisdom into an evolved, unique relationship.

Being constantly online taught the younger generations problem-solving awareness and discernment. They have excellent recommendations for parents, and when embraced as an adult, unique relationships seed and grow. For example, many years ago, my husband asked for a new Walkman to play his music while exercising. Our teenage girls sweetly smiled and said, "Daddy, let's get your favorite songs added into a playlist app on your phone as a customized library." Genius! Now, whenever we seek a technology upgrade, we first seek our adult daughters' counsel or their boyfriends for the best high-tech approach. Likewise, when they need financial or relationship advice, they ask us. Friendships deepen when both sides express value and gratitude towards another's skills and talents.

What is horrifically painful is when either side feel rejected because no transition happened. It can suddenly occur when the daughter or son feels controlled or minimized by their parents. They seek a friendship in their parents that never became a reality. The result is not pleasant. A parent is left clueless when their grown child ghosts them, quits communicating, and fades away. It is heartbreaking. If that has happened, muster the courage to stay positive and pray for their return to your family. Ask God to give you the perspective of what caused them to distance themselves. Try to understand their need for a boundary between you. Your heart may ache, but never stop believing you will reconcile with your child. Be consistent in your message that you are there and love them. Tell yourself it is a temporary situation to ease your fear; this won't last forever. Pray for direction on how to establish a connection where both feel loved and respected. Be emotionally prepared to alter your parental relationship to more of a friendship when you see them in the future.

Our middle daughter Elle was 19 years old when she brought the need for a transition into focus. She sweetly smiled and pointed out I was being overly helpful. She was a grown woman handling life's challenges in her way. Her words made me realize our relationship was changing. "Mom, I got this. If I need some help, you'll be the first I'll ask. I love you." Those words helped me see her less as a child and more as a social equal.

Reality hit hard. It was time to step back from parenting and recognize her as an adult with whom I should forge a friendship. Was it easy? No way! Next time I thought she might need help, I learned to ask in this manner, "Do you have this?" Our way to recognize her independence was to let her know support was available if she wanted it.

TRUTH BOMB:

Sometimes, hanging on when instead it is time to let go can be just as destructive as letting go when it is time to hang on.

Aging Mother-Daughter

In the summer, I took my mother for a routine exam. She felt and looked great, bouncing into the doctor's office. It was a shock when they sent her to the hospital for an elevated pulse. In one hour, our whole lives changed for the worse. Five months later, we were both exhausted, and it showed. I felt washed out and frustrated, literally, to tears from all the caregiving. I admit that I sat on my deck many days looking at the sunset, drinking a cold beer, tears dripping off my cheeks. I had lost all control in my life and in helping hers. No matter what I did to help, it did not seem like enough in Mom's journey for healing. I unrealistically and impatiently wanted her to bounce back and feel like herself again. Yet over the months, we learned to forge a new understanding. I finally agreed to see her as "old."

What a moment of truth. As a child, I don't think any of us are prepared to accept the biological fact that our revered parents are actually old. Mom kept saying that she was old over the last two years, and I would not listen.

My reply was, "You are not old; you are getting older." Then when all this hit, I finally saw my amazing mom as frail and aged. It had to be noticeable, like a ton of wet sand poured on my head to reach that realization. Our relationship went from being social equals to an aging mother's caregiver. I was not fond of this new dynamic and was not accepting of it. I worried, fretted, and cried in private. Did those wasted emotions help? No. They consumed, confused, and drained me even more. I wanted our former lives back, and that was not logically going to happen. Talk about being in denial.

I share this story not to highlight my suffering but to increase your awareness of how easy it is to become self-absorbed during a crisis. As humans, we get sucked into our duties while failing to notice a transition. I was late for the transition phase. My mom needed a friend during her lonely days of recovery. She did not need an overly doting worried caregiver.

If you are going through a situation like this, here are some suggestions for making the transition with an elderly person into a friendship mode:

- Keep your focus on that person's overall happiness. It is not just about their physical health.
- Pretend that person is your best friend and treat them with that different mindset.
- Be present. Don't try to multi-task and exhaust yourself.
- Aim to connect deeper with who they are. Let them talk about things they care about.
- Find what will make them smile more so you feel joy too.
- Discover what you can do to bring joy into their daily life.
- Ask, "Is there a favorite dessert you haven't had in a while?"
- Leave a radio playing their favorite music, so they hear something familiar and pleasing.
- Watch a favorite show together—it's about companionship.
- Release yourself from the heavy responsibility to "fix what you want their world to look like."
- Remember, it is about what they want. Including their lifestyle and household belongings.
- Don't rearrange things without their permission.
- Be patient and respectful when reacting.

A friend would not be overly demanding or declarative about what the older person should or should not do anymore. A friend would word it as concern and suggest things to help make their life easier. That blunder is where most aging parent relationships fail is to transition into friendship. Here is a good thing to remember. An aging parent with a sound mind is not usually ready to surrender their independence and submit to your plans. Yet frequently, the well-meaning daughter (or son) enters with an "I will take over the situation" mindset. That is not their role! The parent needs a friend and an advocate for their care.

Advocacy means to make sure the aging parent is treated well with kindness, love, and friendship. Just like how a parent needs to let a child grow up, the child needs to honor the parent and not treat them as a child when they are elderly.

 TIPS:

- Be the person your mom or dad wants to spend some time with and not the doting/demanding daughter or son.
- Stop focusing on cleaning the house and reorganizing based on how you think it needs to look.
- Stay engaged as a best friend would and enjoy the relationship as it transitions to friendship.
- Focus on laughing more together and find ways that can bring joy into their final years.

Diminished Aging Parent - Reality Check

Sometimes, we have to witness another's situation to awaken us to see the goodness in our daily life. One day, as I sat in the doctor's office waiting for my mom to finish with the specialist, I met a striking older blonde named Donja. She was waiting for her 94-year-old mother to be transported over from the nursing home. Since COVID-19 hit, she could no longer visit her mom or take her to appointments. I saw how Donja felt robbed of the frequent chance to see her mom in person at her facility. Instead, Donja had to wait in the doctor's lobby to catch a few moments with her mom, Mildred. Her stylish mom rolled in with help from an aide. Donja and her looked more like beautiful sisters. Her mom was a knock-out with a huge smile, yet I noticed a lack of warmth when seeing Donja.

The mom sat emotionless and kept asking why the chairs were taped with "do not sit" signs. Suddenly, her mom's Alzheimer's became obvious. It dawned on me that these sweet ladies' situations and relationships had transitioned over the decades. Donja, her devoted daughter, missed the engaged mom who raised her. Donja had now become her mom's friend. The pandemic limited them from seeing each other daily as before, which robbed Donja of seeing her mom on her lucid days. How sad for them both. What a reality check this was for me. I wanted my mom physically to be her former vibrant self, and instead, these ladies had an extreme version of a situationally induced relationship. They did not even get a choice. Life transitioned their worlds for them.

There is always someone suffering more. Seeing a worse situation usually shakes us hard enough to realize we have few problems. No matter how bad our world feels, we need to make ourselves stop and find the beauty of our existing relationships. That lady had no idea what lesson she taught me that day. My Mom would improve physically and thankfully had her mental clarity intact. Our good days were right now transitioning from our mother – daughter relationship into a deeper friendship.

 TIP:

I firmly believe it is our responsibility to pay attention to what God reveals. The next time you observe someone dealing with a similar situation, consider if you are being sent a message. It could be your reality check.

While *Collecting True Friends,* remember to look for *situational friendships* and include those nearby. The relationships you had in the past do not have to be the same types as in your future. You have a choice of how, when, and if, you want friendships to evolve. Be open to those including the elderly, a parent, relative, neighbor, the disabled, military buddy, mentor, an animal, club member, or someone younger. A beautiful friendship may just evolve into something fun that you never even imagined possible.

Next, we will be exploring more ways to be a true friend and what that means during times of stress or struggles. True friends are not just there for fair weather days but in life's ups and downs, too. What should you expect from your friends during such times? Let's move on digging deeper how you can build friendship making and keeping skills in the upcoming lessons regarding how life happens.

CHAPTER 10
LIFE HAPPENS – ALLEVIATING STRESSORS & SUFFERING

True friends pull each other to the shore when life feels like a shipwreck. The ability to recognize a friend's needs differentiates the fair-weather friend from the real deal. Friends don't always feel comfortable expressing embarrassment or emotional pain. How so? It requires sharing something kept inside and admitting they can't move beyond it in the moment. A family issue, illness, or workplace strife can be so stressful they slowly shut down. Some call it, going into their own bubble. We all saw a lot of bubbles worldwide happening during the pandemic period. For example, I've watched friends isolate themselves after being fired by their employer. Another good friend disappeared from my inner circle when her teenage son and his unsavory friends were arrested and faced trial.

"I'm Fine"

How can you make sure you are more than a fair-weather friend to inner circle friends? Start by being more aware if you haven't heard from a member of your inner circle in a while. If you've known a friend long enough, you will recognize patterns in how frequently you talk. When it's been too long, intuition may tell you your friend needs help. They may be suffering. If so, find ways to engage. It is not ideal to wait until your friend contacts you for help. Why? Because they usually won't unless they are accustomed to asking for help. If they are traditionally the giver in an inner circle, they may not even know how to ask for help. Ironically, the stronger a person is, the more they need their friends to offer help when they suffer. Our society has become hyper-focused on helping the person who complains the loudest or is underserved. As noble as this habit may seem, the strongest also suffer and should never be ignored because we think "they'll be alright." So often those are the people who followed the harsh mandates given as a kid to "walk it off" or "suck it up buttercup." As adults, they are the ones that respond now with "I'm fine" when they are not fine! That's where being a true friend requires that you apply yourself with consistency to everyone in your inner circle. If someone is acting outside of their normal behavior, then everything is NOT fine. It is up to you to take the initiative, even if it seems somewhat invasive. Be the person to ask to see your friend. You might ask if you can send over a home cooked meal, cut their grass, take the kids off their hands, walk their dog, or another thoughtful offer to engage.

Thank You for Understanding I'm Hurting – Marlie's Story
Here is an example of when to make time to listen with empathy to a suffering friend. This conversation happened during a friendly "checking-in" phone call. I sensed something was weird even though my friend Marlie denied it. Three times she said, "I am fine." She casually mentioned her parents were not well.

I gently pushed her to tell me more about her ailing parent's situation. I said, "I have the time right now to listen . . . would you please tell me how YOU are feeling. I want to help. Please talk to me."

In reading this following conversation, mentally note how it makes you feel. Check your awareness if you sense the depth of suffering revealed by my friend as she uncorked her emotions.

Marlie continued by saying, "Thank you for really listening to what's going on with my family; they are making me #$*&#% crazy. I never know what is going to happen next! Will they set the house on fire? Or clog up the pipes, or microwave a pot? Mom fired all the caregivers again last week. I get it. They want to be in charge and live independently. Mom is angry about her world, and now dementia is slowly creeping in. Daily it's getting worse, and I am afraid of what might go wrong next. It's heartbreaking. The worst part of it all is she has no kindness for me or my brothers, only contempt. It is all about her 24/7 without any love for us kids." Marlie paused and started to sob.

Then she loudly vented, "Thanks for listening. I mean it. Thank you! You are the FIRST person who listened to ME. Everyone else told me how I should feel or rambled about what else I needed to do for Mom as they did for their parents. I'm about to retire in two years, and this should be a happy time in my life . . . it should be about my husband and me. Instead, I got nothing but a hot mess around me. Dealing with all of this just really sucks!"

I understood Marlie's struggle and conflict to love her parents but hate being the appointed head caregiver. I had some point of reference to offer genuine empathy. Back in 2004, my father had an unexpected stroke and his medical arrangements fell on my mom and me. We spent a horrible 14 months until he passed. Here are my words that helped Marlie's breathe for a moment. I said, "You probably feel like you are going in circles; your mom's situation keeps changing, and it's exhausting! She has kind words for strangers and none for you. Your mom puts on a show of her independence, firing the help. Her actions then create another bomb for you to diffuse. She probably says, "No one is doing enough for me or appreciates me."

"Yes!! That's it." Marlie said. "How in the world did you know my mom said I wasn't doing enough for her? It hurts so bad when she says these terrible things to me and Dad just shakes his head while she fusses. We have tried so hard to do all the right things. My family's lives are on hold."

Is There Any Difference Between Sympathy and Empathy?
Sympathy is showing you are aware or understand that someone is suffering. Empathy requires an emotional connection, usually from having already experienced such pain. For example, I can be sympathetic to someone who has broken their arm and try to be thoughtful about how to help them during recovery. I cannot be fully empathetic since I have never broken a bone. However, when it comes

to grief over the death of a significant loved one, I am highly experienced and able to be 100% empathetic.

Marlie just needed to know she was heard and not feel judged. Have you ever wanted to talk with someone you thought would listen to you yet departed disappointed because they failed to relate? Or you had a conversation with an acquaintance and felt surprising joy when you discovered they possessed genuine empathy. Everyone has experienced difficult times with families, careers, health, finances, faith, relationships, and needed to talk to help feel relief. Having a conversation is like a tennis game requiring two people. It's hard to feel comforted if no one is listening. Since you are on a journey to collect true friends worthy of your time and devotion, another key skill to master is being attentive. We've talked a great deal about using your awareness to spot potential friends. Now it is time to discuss the ability to see and listen to those suffering. Why is this important? Because attentiveness can make or break a friendship. Remember, a true friend is not just for fair weather days. Let me say this again, a true friend pulls each other to the shore when life feels like a shipwreck.

Remember What Others Value – Be the Real Deal

If you are tech-friendly, load onto your phone calendar dates that are important to your friends so you can remember to follow up. For example, birthdays, anniversaries, graduations, weddings, births, deaths of loved ones, milestones, etc. If that is too difficult, buy a paper calendar and start marking those dates down. Then next year, transfer all those dates to your new calendar. Before an event happens, send a text or card, make a phone call, or communicate in any thoughtful way to let your friend know they are remembered. What is important to your true friend should also be important to you!

Listen More and Avoid This Mistake

A common conversational mistake is echoing what your friend says instead of being truly empathic. For example, you say your dog died and your friend says, "Oh yes, I remember when my dog died, I this, I that, me, me, me, me . . . ." That is not empathy. When the friend responding takes the opportunity to ramble on about the death of their beloved pet, they are making it all about themselves. Why? Even though both friends lost their beloved pets, the first was a recent loss and emotions were fresh. The person currently suffering needs to be the primary focus during the conversation.

So, what should you do when talking to someone dealing with a significant life issue? I recommend another approach. Let's look at this example and why it works. If your friend is unexpectedly fired or laid off, be attentive to how their emotional recovery will come in waves. A layered approach of understanding works best. First, they will be in shock. What should your response be? Realize you can see the bigger picture because you are not the one physically or emotionally compromised. It is not the right time to talk about all the things (good and bad) while their trauma feels that fresh. The suffering friend is operating with compromised thinking. Instead, write down some notes to talk about later when you realize your friend is mentally ready. Talking about any of those things now will not relate well to their needs or help with emotional recovery. For example, they may be primarily concerned about what their friends at work will think. They didn't even get to say goodbye. It is a personal loss at this point, or they lack enough current skills to be employed.

Be a friend that realizes they need time to work through the disappointment, shock, and embarrassment of being let go by their company. What else should you do?

- Pay careful attention to what they say. Their chosen words reveal deeper emotions than they may be aware of. For example, if they say, "I thought I'd be working there another four years until my car is paid off." That is a clue they had a mental plan, and they may have financial concerns.

- Ask your upset friend, "Are you just venting, or do you want my advice?" Most of the time, you will find out they just are venting. That means you don't have to have any advice or answers on how they could fix the situation. All you have to do is nod and actively listen.

- Offer to buy them dinner at a location where you both can sit awhile to talk openly.

- If they want to be alone, tell them you will call them tomorrow and plan to see them in the next two days. Remember to allow time in your calendar to do the follow up.

- If they are a hugger, hug them and say, "I am so sorry this has happened to you—remember, I will be here to help." They probably don't need to figure anything else out tonight or tomorrow.

- Invite them to take some deep breaths with you before walking away.

- Give them a gleam of hope. Assure them that what they are living through will not continue forever, even though it feels like a dark eternity. Your friend needs to believe one day it will get easier.

 TIP:

Sharing a pain experience can bond friends. It is appropriate to share your hard learned lessons but remember to not focus too much about yourself. It is vital to let them see the real you who recovered through a struggle. It allows them to feel the emotions from your past during a painful time.

It's Hard to Be Vulnerable

For too long, I carried conflicted emotions on how I felt about my father. I loved him, but I also was disappointed how he was constantly abrupt with others. We lived for decades with his drinking problem and had to keep it a secret to protect his security clearance. For years, I naively prayed God could make him stop drinking. When he finally quit drinking five years later, he had a massive stroke. Unbelievably and to his benefit, after his stroke, people pitied him, thinking his rudeness stemmed from the stroke. Wow! Ironic, right? If they had known the truth. Daddy is gone, and I no longer keep the secret of how painful it was living with an alcoholic. How do I share this truth to help others? When appropriate, I share the hurt and conflict my family endured when I hear someone too embarrassed to talk about alcoholism because they feel no one would understand. It has been cathartic to several friends and colleagues who said, "We had no idea you suffered from this family dynamic, too. If your family got through this, I now have hope we can too."

Even though caring for a loved-one is the right thing to do, it doesn't mean you have to like them as a person. Forgive them, yes. Love them, hopefully. But you do not have to like them as a person if their values are incompatible with yours. When we deny the truth inside of us about disliking someone or something, it can make us feel guilty. In Marlie 's story above, perhaps her mom was not a nurturer and not much love remained for her children. In those situations, what is the best thing you can do to help your friend suffering? Acknowledge she can confide her feelings to you, and you won't judge her. Make it sound logical. Tell her you can't judge her since you have not lived her life or been in that situation.

Friendship Creed
- Keep your word! If you learn something in confidence from your friend or their terrible situation they are dealing with, you must honor your promise to treat it confidentially.
- If you say you will be there, be there. Do not be the person who constantly reschedules. Your friend may have planned to talk with you, and now they will go unheard.
- The creed requires you to treasure your true friendship first and honor your word!

Love On the Caregivers

It is an endless job being a caregiver. Truth Bomb: everyone always asks about the patient, and few see the exhausted, conflicted zombie standing right in front of them. Many caregivers are women and usually mothers. If one of those is your friend, that's a tight spot for them to be juggling work, kids, home, spouse, church, pets, neighbors, school, plus a patient. They may have little or no self-care time. That's where having a great friend can provide some relief—setting a regular time to walk or drop off a meal at their home once a week can let your friend breathe. Or even sending a heart-felt card in the mail telling them they are an amazing, beautiful person can make a difference in them realizing they have great value in this world.

 PONDERING PAUSE:

- In my past, have I watched a friend suffer and was confused how to help?
- Knowing what was just covered, if that happened today, what would I do differently to help a friend?
- Can I recall a time when I was in pain or suffering?
- During that time, was I able to share *honestly* with a friend how I felt?
- Do I recall which friends (or people) reached out or helped me recover?
- Am I still in contact with those who helped me? Would I consider reconnecting? If yes, I will say how I was thinking about them and wanted to thank them for being such a great friend when they helped me back then. Plus, I will inquire how they are doing and what's happening in their world now.

Hopefully, you agree that to be a true friend it is necessary to be aware of a friend who is suffering. Remember, the key to relating to their pain is to focus your attention on their situation. Your experience in the past may help you empathize, but don't talk too long about your past even though it seems relatable. Also, do not say things like, "I feel so sorry for you right now." That phrase suggests pity and helplessness. What is ideal is to express sympathy or empathy instead. You could say, "I understand how hard this feels right now; with time; it will get better. Can you think of any way I can help you?" Be reassuring. Make sure you actively listen and give advice or suggestions when asked. Strive to hear the emotions behind their words they choose to speak. The words they say express deeper feelings, so pay close attention.

Here's an interesting thing I find helpful. Say a prayer, or set a positive intention, before you see your distressed friend, of what to say. Ask for the right words to pop into your mind and heart that will bring relief and wisdom to your friend's situation. Then, when talking with your friend, if certain words naturally come to your mind, use those exact words. Surprisingly, those words are usually what your friend needs to hear. It is amazing how goodness can channel through you when you don't block it. When I have felt compelled to say a particular word or phrase with a hurting friend, even though it is not ordinarily in my vocabulary, I later realized that specific word had meaning. I remember one time, my friend looked shocked and smiled like I'd reminded her of something. Then I realized I had been a messenger to share that divinely tailored message from her favorite uncle. Specific words may remind them of something a favorite person said many years ago.

Some of us may be fortunate never to suffer tragedies. During difficult times helping another can make a relationship deeper. If you are the person who endured significant loss, you have my empathy. I recommend you reflect on who was there for you and who was not. Those who were actively helpful need to be remembered and treasured. If you are not still in touch, reach out with gratitude and see if you can reacquaint. It might be a friendship ready to bloom. Those who were not present when you were suffering may need to be reviewed to consider how well they fit in your inner circle.

Random acts of kindness always boomerang back to you somewhere in life. You may not see it, but it is all woven into your personal development and evolution. Acts of kindness are cumulative and will help you become the best version of yourself. When your happiness shines, more true friends will be attracted to you. Being a constant and loving friend demonstrates you are worthy of having true friends. That may all sound a little "woo-woo," yet it is the truth.

Your journey commenced with *Collecting True Friends* and has gone even deeper into the mechanics of how to be a great friend to others. Another friendship-making talent to learn is the ability to spot from a distance someone in need. It can be a challenge because many potential friends and your inner circle may try to camouflage their world when they are distressed. If you learn how to take action, you can strategically position yourself into their life to be their friend, giving them the right uplift. Everyone needs help some time in their life, and those who develop the trained eye and ears to spot those in need are the ones bountiful in devoted friends. Let's continue how to develop those skills in our next chapter.

CHAPTER 11
SPOTTING WHEN TO HELP – BE THE REAL DEAL

Friendship Making and Keeping Skills You've Learned So Far

You are doing great! We've covered so much information, lessons, stories, pondering pauses, and 'aha' moments. Together we've worked through this layered learning approach so you can become a fantastic true friend who will attract the same. Before we move on to learning how to spot when to help a friend, let's refresh our memories on the tools you have gained:

- Awareness of those people in your inner circle
- Awareness of those you meet or are nearby
- Discernment used as a powerful tool to see others
- Applying discernment with awareness to locate potential quality friends easier
- Inventory of who's in your inner circle
- Consideration of who may no longer be a good fit
- The benefits of collecting a variety of types of friends with varied traits
- Using your desired qualities list as your guide for who gets into your inner circle
- Intentionally looking for people with those desired qualities
- Understanding how obstacles block connecting
- Stopping roadblocks (in you or others) from preventing friendships from advancing
- Social media techniques to improve your communications
- In-person techniques to improve your communications
- How to be the "real deal" that is a magnet for more true friends
- Modifying ill-serving behaviors that keep people from connecting with you deeper
- Ways to help a suffering or stressed friend recover and what you should expect

Now is a great time to dive deeper to learn additional skills to become the real deal and be a true friend in return. Communication etiquette with friends and colleagues is more than saying please and thank you. Learning the art of proper etiquette is a skill set that, when mastered, will help you every day and everywhere. For example, etiquette includes refining and choosing one's messaging styles when mixing with varied groups (friends, coworkers, neighbors). It also requires active listening to hear someone in need and know when to become their resource. The skill you will develop is the ability to *spot* someone in need and not overlook their issue because you are preoccupied or believe "I should mind my own business." True friendships grow and thrive when the right amount of help is extended. Again, there is an art of spotting and knowing when to be of assistance.

I have heard this said over and over: "We are no longer friends because that person knew what I was dealing with and wasn't there in my time of need. They didn't even bother to ask how I was dealing with that horrible time." As we've discussed, many friendships do not survive when a friend fails to act in a manner considered acceptable by the other. It can happen because they don't listen enough or do something rude, especially when a friend is hurting and ignored, or feel neglected by a friend who could have helped but did not. That is why being able to spot an ideal time to help can keep and anchor a friendship. For example, during the summer, Donna's air conditioning died, and she didn't have the money at the moment to fix the central air. Her friend Keagan insisted she take his portable window unit for immediate relief. Plus, he arranged for his handyman to install it the next morning. That is the ability to spot a need and proactively be present for a true friend in need before their stress rises higher. If that person would do it for you, it is a no-brainer to step up and offer them help if it is within your powers.

Stress is one of the biggest obstacles that block our way to practice being more aware. When stressed with too much on our plates, tunnel vision can result as a personal coping mechanism. We tend to put on our "air masks first before we help others," as said on airplanes. Focusing on our own needs and deadlines minimizes our ability to stay aware of friends in need. Being an overachiever, I support the need to hit personal goals. However, we also must accept that not everything in life stays on schedule. Your plans can be interrupted by someone in need. It might be a friend, potential friend, colleague, neighbor, family member, acquaintance, or even an animal in distress.

Releasing yourself from a rigid mindset, "if it's not on my schedule, it will wait," can create the positive energy needed to sprout a potential friendship. Can you consider accepting a more flexible mindset? Here is the flip side to ignoring a friend who needs your attention. If you aren't flexible to stop and help others in need, you limit asking them to help you. Have you heard how the law of reciprocity works? It is about sowing seeds in others. Seeds are your natural gifts, talents, resources, wisdom, or mentorship. I've listened to many people that wish to gain better friends or build a loyal business network, yet they ignore reciprocity. As a result, they fail to sow seeds in their community. Lack of awareness is usually the reason they missed spotting how to help. It all goes back to the biblical lesson about reaping what you sow.

Awareness, Ability to Listen, and Accessibility
I want to dive deeper into using your awareness skills to help you "show up" as the real deal to others. Let's explore specific skills to help you become a true friend worthy of other faithful friends. This is when awareness, ability to listen, and accessibility become the dominant traits for learning and implementing.

We sow seeds early because we plan for a harvest later. Right? It requires planning, and as with any good plan, it can be interrupted. That's how it works in friendship building too. Our awareness can start in high-beam mode and fade away from lack of use or distractions. The story of Kimberly, my colleague, who I felt compelled to befriend even though she was suspicious of my intentions, is a great example. Awareness allowed me to spot a need in her, even if I did not know her exact need. I was sure one day we should get to know one another better. Even though her friendship awareness radar was off, I remained patient. Kimberly needed a good friend. It was up to me to seed a friendship because she couldn't envision it. That was why Kimberly lacked a quality inner circle. Later, when her awareness increased, she understood she needed to collect more healthy friends and directly asked for my help.

Awareness and Ability (to Listen)

Awareness and an ability to stop long enough to listen to others are fundamental skills to develop if your desire is to make and keep true friends. It is what distinguishes the casual friend of convenience from the real deal friend. Have you ever witnessed a broken-down car jamming up traffic and the horns start blowing? Honking a horn is not helpful. Some Samaritans spot the stalled car and physically push the vehicle to a safer spot to clear the lane. Everyone notices they were helpful because traffic flows again. They became aware of the problem and acted. Their actions were appreciated by all impacted. This analogy shows that by training yourself to observe people and occurrences more keenly, you'll know better how to make a positive difference (sowing a seed).

Accessibility

If being aware and listening are the beginning steps towards making genuine friends, accessibility is the next important step towards being the real deal. Accessibility works both ways. It would help if you were accessible to your friends, and they need to be accessible for you to reach them. Have you ever tried repeatedly to catch up with someone for a quick talk, and they don't text or call back? How did that feel after a few days passed? Probably not good. You begin to wonder why they haven't called back or won't pick up the phone or return your text. We've all been there! You might think everyone is swamped. So, you patiently wait while hearing "crickets." Then later, you read a social media post showing a fun outing they shared with other friends. That makes you think deeper. Suddenly you believe you are not a priority in that person's life. Or that's the story that whispers in your mind. Yet, it could be that it was a work-related event they had to attend.

That's why accessibility is essential when you are building relationships and want to keep them thriving. Actions speak louder than words. If no one can reach you and there is no follow-up, you will fall off their radar. Eventually, after many requests, a friend fades away. Was it an unexpected loss or a benefit? Was that person supposed to become a true lifetime friend, but you failed to engage enough? When that happens to me, I reflect on whether that person leaving my circle was supposed to.

 PONDERING PAUSE:

Thinking about your awareness ability and accessibility- answer the following questions:

- On a scale of 1–10, how do I rate my awareness level of people overall? _____ friends? ___
- Do I stop long enough to listen to an acquaintance? (1–10) ___
- Do I stop and listen enough to someone in my inner circle? (1–10) ___
- Am I generally accessible when others try to connect? (1–10)_____
- How well do I follow up when someone reaches out to me? (1–10) _____

Take Time to Amplify Your Awareness – Be the Real Deal

A networking buddy of mine, LaTasha, texted asking if I'd call her after lunch for some advice. I thought the topic would be related to my consulting and training services. I was unaware she needed personal advice. When she answered, I heard her frantic voice. "Thanks for calling me. I'm at the end of my rope and can't take it anymore; I need a woman's advice. I'm the only person left in my family that hasn't abandoned my daughter. She's become nothing but a huge problem since she's moved home. My life is total chaos. I don't know where to turn." When I heard the grief and mother's conflicted emotions in her voice, I quickly realized this would be an entirely different type of call. I spotted her need and put down everything around me to fully listen.

 PONDERING PAUSE:

Remember when an acquaintance or colleague (someone not yet a close friend) asked to talk or asked for advice. Reflect on how that felt and ask yourself these questions.

- Was I surprised they were talking to me about that situation? ___Yes ___ No
- Did I stop enough to fully listen? ___Yes ___ No
- Did it seem like us talking helped? ___Yes ___ No
- Were they open to my suggestions? ___ Yes ___ No
- Did they need a safe place to vent? ___ Yes ___ No
- Did I follow up later to see how they were doing? ___ Yes ___ No

LaTasha continued talking for five solid minutes without pause. I let her talk and listened, holding myself back from interrupting. Her lifestyle had dramatically changed in the last year. She'd been trapped for months working remotely from home with a grown woman causing her angst and disruptions. She felt isolated and overwhelmed. Since I was a mother of three, LaTasha knew I could empathize with her heartfelt dilemma to evict her disruptive daughter. We covered the basic options like boundaries and counseling to help with the root of her issues. Counseling had helped before. What I did not hear in her conversation is if she had requested divine assistance. We'd never talked about her faith before. Finally, however, I felt compelled to ask. "Have you asked above for some help?"

There was a pause, and she slowly said, "Every time I asked, I would get so frustrated because it felt more like I was giving God my wish list rather than talking. So, I stopped asking a while back."

We have all been there! We get out of the habit of seeking help from others on earth as well as from above. Especially the strongest people with heavy loads forget to seek help. They act like pack mules. Life gets busy, and those healthy habits, like eating right, praying, and walking, fade away. We don't deliberately choose to stop the positive habits. It's like remembering to drink more water to stay hydrated. We must make a conscious effort and time every day to keep that habit. LaTasha had forgotten to ask for help, and prayer was no longer a habit. Yet, she was aware to reach out to me as a trusted resource for a heartfelt conversation and help. That was a great start!

Life gets crazy busy, and it's easy to forget we can ask for help from above plus from our trusted allies and friends. Instead, we fool ourselves, believing we can fix it on our own. Yet even animals have friends and act visibly happy, wagging their tails when they see one another. Friendship with compassion is one of the most beautiful resources that humankind has here on Earth. It reminds us we are not alone, and someone cares. When we hurt, knowing that someone stopped to listen and tried to uplift us is a powerful feeling! One of the jewels that makes you the real deal friend and very different from others is the ability to stop, listen, and be compassionate.

As you consciously work to *Collect True Friends,* make a point to practice awareness of those in need. LaTasha was in need. She felt used by her daughter, abandoned by God, and all that remained were endless piles of work. She lost her joy along the way. I realized how deeply she must have placed her trust in me to share the hurt. I felt honored she'd ask for my counsel. She probably mentally ran through a list of contacts who could offer a woman and mother's perspective. Then she landed on my name. Our phone time together deepened our regard for one other. We were not only colleagues, but along the way, we became friends.

Before we hung up, I shared my mother's favorite easy prayer to use in times of confusion. "God, show me the way." I asked her to say it five times daily, especially when stressed. Then, I explained by asking for favor, she will stay open to the possibility of receiving help. The next day, I sent an audio text of me praying, mentioning specific details we'd discussed.

TIP:

Recording your voice and then texting a voice message conveys your heartfelt tone within your message on a deeper level.

LaTasha needed to know someone *spotted* she needed help. She needed to know she was heard, and someone was concerned about her heartache. Using your increased awareness skill plus making the time on your busy calendar is what makes you the real deal. That is how you will "show up" as a true friend.

> *"Wise Men Don't Need Advice. Fools Won't Take It."*
> ~ *Benjamin Franklin*

Another thing to learn is when not to offer your help. This can be the case when a friend, family member, or colleague would prefer to hear the advice they want, not the advice they need, or when they trust someone who has less experience and knowledge than you do. I can think of four things that might be happening when this aggravating circumstance occurs:

- They don't see you as a resource to help on that subject.
- They forgot or never knew you had experience in that area.

- They are intimidated by you and don't want to seem less knowledgeable.
- Their ego doesn't allow them to be less informed, showing a highly competitive nature roadblocking their growth.

Allow *Space and Grace t*o Others

It's like parenting a teenager and how they ignore your guidance. Then they later mention they accepted poor advice from someone else. The only thing you can do is give them space and grace to learn and seek better counsel next time. You allow them space and grace to be more aware to discern where they seek advice. What do you do when someone you care about ignores your help or advice? The first thing is never to say, "I told you so." The best approach is to smile and wish them well, finding a good answer, then recite Ben Franklin's quote to yourself, "Wise Men Don't Need Advice. Fools Won't Take It." Also, that's when I would go enjoy a cold beer to let go! Ben would have liked that too, I'm sure.

Eleanor's Cry for Help

It was a beautiful spring day in Virginia Beach. The four of us, Ted and Claudia, my husband, and I were going to the Aviation Museum to enjoy an annual flying event. There would be food, music, historical displays, and vintage aircraft flying. At the last moment, a fifth person asked to come along and meet some new friends, the adorable Eleanor 'Elle.' I never imagined five years later it would result in her fairy tale wedding at the same location from the love we witnessed bloom on this day.

Here's what happened. While the guys pumped gas, the three of us ladies had a private girls' talk in the back seat. Elle confided how fortunate she thought we were to have loving husbands. She slowly lifted her head and shared that she wanted to find love with someone special too. She wanted her loneliness to end. I didn't know Elle very well, but I could tell from her intensity that she was sincere in her desire to find love. I looked into her big eyes and asked if she had ever proclaimed specifically aloud what she wanted in life. She had not. "Asking for divine help in this big universe is 'Step One' in any dilemma," I gently revealed.

As we sat in the backseat of the car waiting for the guys to return, we repeated a mantra, "I will meet an amazing man worthy of me. God help me." We agreed that Claudia and I would help her meet some new friends over the coming months while looking for love.

By noon we were at the airfield. We walked Elle over to the crowd and discussed where to begin. We soon discovered she lacked the confidence and didn't know how to start or what to say with men. We giggled like schoolgirls about how married women would help her (the single lady) flirt. We modeled how to stand to appear inviting and offered some phrases to start conversations. The three of us glided through the crowd, introducing Elle to fellow spectators. She smiled and practiced her new "flirting" skills and built up her confidence. Then a wonderful thing happened. Elle was actually in the right place at the right time. That's what many call "God's Wink." Several pilots were sitting and standing in a group. Claudia introduced Elle to a single pilot named Mike. That's when the magic started. It was like watching a flower bloom in slow motion. Elle had sincerely asked for help. She became highly favored. She proclaimed she was ready to meet an amazing man, and Mike (for some reason, he still doesn't understand) stayed an hour longer than usual at the Aviation Museum. Had he left on time they would never have met. I know why it happened. She asked for help, and the timing was right to receive.

It was now 3:00 p.m. Elle and Mike made plans to see each other again, and everyone went home. I did not see much of Elle after that but heard how happy Elle and Mike were traveling on their adventures. The couple spent more and more time together and grew closer and closer. Now, fast-forward five years later, we danced at their gorgeous wedding. The stunning, beaming bride Eleanor pulled me aside from the receiving line and whispered into my ear, "Because of YOU, I'm getting married today. Thank you so much for helping me ask for love."

My heart pounded with joy, as tears filled my eyes. What a lovely thing to say about my part in making that blessing happen. Eleanor became a pilot, too, like her hubby Mike. They share a passion for everything in the aviation world. Even the wedding cake was decorated with maps and airplanes. Mike never thought he'd meet a woman who loved his hobby and him so much. She is his soul mate. It was a real-life Cinderella story, and they are living happily ever after.

Cupid's Bow
Trusting her friends and expressing her desire to find love and being open to ask for help was a profound turning mark in Elle's life. Her ability and willingness to listen and pray is why this story has such a great ending. As a bonus, we all witnessed that listening to a friend in need and knowing WHEN to offer assistance is critical. This story shows *spotting a friend in need* and taking action can often achieve remarkable results. You can't argue with success.

 PONDERING PAUSE:

Answer what you think would have happened if Eleanor "Elle" had not been open to:
- A change in her life to end her loneliness
- Trusting her friends
- Asking her friends for *specific* help
- Trying something different (like praying with a specific intent to receive)
- Taking action by implementing tactics shared by her trusted friends to improve her ability to talk with strangers.

Action Items:

- What area of your life do you want to change?
- Which of your friends can you trust to share your desire and ask for help?
- Do any of your friends have the:
  - expertise (or track record) to help guide you to change.
  - resources (time, support, money, connections).
  - willingness to help you reach that goal.

Once you've identified a list of the friends (or connections) who would be ideal to talk with, here's what to do next. First, reach out to ask if they could speak for 15–30 minutes about something on your mind. Then, tell them you would welcome their thoughts.

 TIP:

It is ideal to be in person (or virtually on camera) so you both can read body language. Your goal when reaching out is to get a time set to talk later. Texting is a great way to achieve that goal. Also, I have learned not to surprise someone with a lengthy text discussion about changes desired in your future. Why? Because most likely, you will not have their full attention. It is best to water-drop a topic to make it interesting. They may even do a little research before your scheduled meetup. If you meet somewhere, pick up the bill because you asked for the meeting. During your meeting, remind them why you selected them to share this conversation for their valued input or direction.

 **NOTE:**

The first person you asked to help may not be the one who is your final best resource. If they are, then you are a winner! If not, consider the first person as good practice for sharing your message. Talking aloud always helps strengthen your courage and be clearer to articulate your deep desire. In addition, you can sense how they respond to you to what you want to happen in your future. Then you can assess if they can be supportive or resourceful with that goal.

 TIP:

If you cannot list anyone's name to ask for help, write down that as something to fix in your life. Declare that you desire to collect a TRUE friend. That will create the opening for that person to come into your life.

In both stories, friends asked for help. What if someone does not ask? In those times, aim to pay attention to spot a friend in need. Remember, not everyone will ask for help. The strongest people are often ignored the most by others who could help. Why? Because others see what's going on and think, "They've got it all worked out. They're fine."

What they don't need is a cheerleader telling them they always succeed and "good luck." Being a strong person, I can share this to be the truth. When a friend notices that I am struggling and is concerned, an ideal opening line would be, "How may I help?" Lengthy stories about their same journey are not usually helpful. Most of the time, a genuine, empathetic offer to help me feels like a warm embrace. Often that is all the help needed. It reminds me that I can call upon them for help when I determine how they can assist. It is a powerful reassurance knowing others have your back and are ready to stand tall next to you. Suddenly you don't feel alone, and it gives you the strength of will, to face the challenges.

Role Model What You Want Friends to Be
Be the real deal of what a true friend does, and it will attract those same people your way. If you have experience working through life challenges and can offer a positive direction to benefit someone

potentially, that background makes you an ideal resource. What is not helpful is when others want to give counsel yet have limited experience on a subject.

Where will you spot someone in need? You've probably noticed the posts on Facebook with friends posting their struggles to figure something out. It does not have to be something too personal. It could be a fun thing like finding a new car or stressful like a family issue. Sometimes people seek information and other times compassion to fix their struggle. If you've championed through a challenge or something you've researched, that information beautifully prepares you to help another facing the same. Or listen closer within your inner circle for someone dealing with what they consider a challenge.

If you have experience, here are example areas you might *spot* a friend to help:
- Financial: debt, planning, college expenses, retirement confusion
- Exercise, cooking, nutrition, fitness
- Relationships – love, friends, family
- Change of life: new community, working from home, relationships, level of faith
- Career, relocation, job transition, retirement, renovation, empty nester to downsize
- Major purchase (car, home, boat, policy, vacation, etc.)
- Loss and grief: deaths, layoffs, betrayals
- Significant events: engagements, babies, marriage, empty nest
- Fun: travel, hobbies, sports, events
- Entrepreneurship: business operations or the emotional roller coaster experience
- Animals or pets

PONDERING PAUSE:

- Which of my friends or connections do I know is dealing with an area listed above?
- Which area do I have training or life experiences in, or make an introduction to someone who can help?
- Which area can I provide a positive direction for that person?
- Is that person aware I am experienced or knowledgeable to help?
- Can I reach out to that person asking if they'd like to talk?

What Stops Others Asking a Question When We Are a Great Resource?

It is surprising how often we hear a friend; family member, neighbor, or colleague tell us about something they've been working through and how they eventually solved it. You listen to how frustrated they were, and all the energy spent to get to the finish line. It surprises you because you had the answer. It's as if you are a math wizard, and someone keeps walking right past you muttering, "If only I knew what 10 x 10 was, then I'd have my answer in life."

You want to jump up and shout, "It's one hundred!" Why does this happen so often?

What stops friends from asking a question when we are a great resource? It's not always because they don't want or aren't open to receiving our help or advice. Many times, it's because we failed to share that we are skilled or experienced in that area. Older people face that a lot when younger people can't imagine them as a master of something in the past. They only see an older person and do not realize the depth of their experiences, knowledge, and relationships. Then a conversation reveals how the more senior person was an expert in their careers, military, raising families, or a pillar in their communities. Expertise can be overlooked and forgotten.

Why don't we fully share what we do and what we know? There are several reasons. One of my friends said, "I don't want to toot my horn and seem like I'm bragging."

I thought, "Seriously?" That knowledge locked down inside her could have saved me dozens of hours of frustration. I had known her for years and would have loved to hear her advice. Yet, I had no idea she possessed the skills I sought. She also did not spot a need in me to offer any assistance.

When we talked about it, I realized her lack of openness to share her talents went back to her early career days. A tyrant boss corrected her sharing behavior. He scolded her, saying, "You are the new person here. I advise you to quit saying so much and showing off how clever you are." He crushed her confidence to mention her talents and abilities.

PONDERING PAUSE:

- I am talented in _____or my skills include _____.

- My friends or colleagues are surprised to find out I am skilled at _____ or interested in learning more about _____.

- I wish my friends and colleagues knew I was amazing at _____.

Shyer people or introverts are often more reserved when mentioning their talents. They may water-drop hints about their abilities, but they usually won't go into detail until a deeper connection and trust gels. So how can you learn what talents others have if they don't openly talk about their experiences? It can be difficult, so here is something proven to try. If invited into someone's home or office, take a moment, and carefully observe what they hang on the walls or collect. It can speak volumes about interests and talents never expressed. Another reason others may keep skills and experience quiet is from fear. Fear of sharing might be interpreted as bragging. So, they hold back from sharing about their awards, hobbies, talents, skills, training, and interests.

Here's a perfect story to show how something in this woman's past restricted her from showing her brilliance. In a convention hall, I met Kindra, and we started talking. I finally extracted that she was an expert on data analytics. I inquired why she hadn't mentioned her extensive training during our group project earlier that day. Our team had struggled for hours sifting through numbers that Kindra could have interpreted simply by looking at the data.

Instead, she quietly sat in the group. She replied, "Elizabeth, nobody wants to hear what I have to say."

I was first stunned, then saddened over Kindra's belief. As a giver, I wanted Kindra to leave feeling better after we talked. I delved a little deeper. "Kindra, you said you believe no one wants to hear what you have to say. Yet, I would have wanted to hear your thoughts, especially since you have expertise. It also would have saved us time at the table." She smiled and looked bewildered. I then asked her if her belief happened in her career or earlier.

"It's been that way since I was a child." That was a light bulb moment for me. I wanted to help her name the root cause of this limiting mindset.

I gently asked, "Kindra, were you told as a child to be quiet?"

She nodded and said, "Yes, in fact, my mum would say, "Kindra, no one wants to hear what you have to say. Go be quiet and play with your toys."

I could feel the sting of her mother's words. They were still deeply rooted as rejection into her heart. I sensed her belief to stay invisible and quiet. It explained why she was dressed all in faded grey matching items, looking like military fatigues.

Before we walked away, I proclaimed to Kindra that she did bring great value and recommended she repeat this message daily, "I help people with my data expertise and know they want to hear what I say." We repeated the phrase together aloud, and then she beamed. It might have been the first time in decades that she'd been seen and heard. The next day, I sat by Kindra, and she engaged with the team during our project. The group smiled and thanked her for contributing her keen insight.

I hope that helps you visualize another opportunity to *spot* someone in need. Kindra didn't ask me directly for help, and I could have easily ignored her sadness. Yet when I saw her hold back her extraordinary talents and expertise from the world and our group, I saw her self-imposed roadblock. We discussed early on how roadblocks and barriers can prevent us from connecting with others. Remember, the person you *spot* to help might be a person possessing the ideal qualities you identified on your friendship qualities list.

Coming up next, we will discover how sharing your talents and skills can make you seem like a rock star in others' eyes. Plus, it will increase your magnetism to attract true friends worthy of your time and devotion.

CHAPTER 12
YOUR TALENTS CAN ACT LIKE A MAGNET
FOR TRUE FRIENDS

A great thing about humans is how we are all so different. No one is identical in processing ideas, learning skills, or evolving. It is fair to say everyone's talents and abilities make them unique. When it comes to making friends, your talents can be your best asset to attract friends. Why? Because your expertise makes you stand out which pulls others closer, much like a magnet. Others are compelled to learn more about you or the talent you possess. You may be skilled at doing something for years that seems routine to you and forget others with limited experience would be intrigued.

Many times, we possess talents or natural abilities that can greatly help a friend. What we possess could bring joy or relief into their lives when shared. However, some humbly regard their knowledge or ability as just ordinary. Later, they are surprised to hear others say they were awe-struck by observing those talents. Those are the occasions that make a person what I affectionately call a "rock star" in someone's eyes. A great blessing may happen next—their relationship catapults from acquaintance to friendship.

We've discussed in detail how to spot someone in need, and now it's time to go bolder in your quest to *Collect True Friends*. It's time to discuss making your expertise known to others. Your extraordinary abilities are a gift and should not remain invisible, especially when you collect friends. A beautiful thing happens when one person shares with their friends something they already enjoy doing. Their friends feel safe asking to join in that activity. When they do, they can determine if it is a good fit for them as well. Casual relationships deepen into stronger friendships by spending time together learning new things. Why? Because both friends are actively engaged in developing new skills at the same time. It creates a memory. The one who is already more experienced gets a chance to be the giver, and the newbie learns from taking instruction. Some fun examples include boating, golfing, cooking, crafting, designing, hobbies, travel, volunteering, and many more activities. It could even include how to go about making new friends, like I do.

Some of us can be reluctant to try something that others have already mastered. It might make them feel embarrassed having to learn something new because they prefer to be what I call "the line leader." A line leader is like the kid in class who enjoyed overseeing and directing classmates. If that feeling of reluctance pops into your heart, take a deep breath and remind yourself you are terrific in different ways. If you don't know how to do something well, don't be shy about asking a friend to teach you. Tell your friend you are interested in learning more about their interest, activity, or subject. Likewise, make sure to invite others to learn new things from you, especially if you spotted their need as discussed in the previous chapter. By boldly communicating you are interested in learning new topics and activities, your inner circle will broaden with interesting people of varied backgrounds. Part of the goal for *Collecting True Friends* is to open your world to include a greater variety of friendships. This is a perfect time to reacquaint yourself with what is missing from your inventory (completed in Chapter 4). You can seek out more of those individual types on your list. Remember, the act of finding friends should result in time spent together being enjoyable.

To locate more desired quality people will require transparency on your side. It means you must be willing to talk about the innate talents or activities you enjoy doing. Whether you are a master or a novice, those unique areas should be shared with your inner circle. I also recommend water-dripping your talents to potential friends while determining if they are a good friendship match. Your hobby might be the thing that resonates most and pulls them closer. Finally, pay close attention to mutual interests since offering to help them may spark the friendship.

TRUTH BOMB:

It is not considered bragging to mention what you find interesting or have experienced. It is unwise to keep your abilities and interests quiet. Why? Because when others discover you are skilled in a subject or activity yet never shared it, they may feel excluded.

Sharing your expertise or talents may include some of these topics:

- Relationship tips
- Health experiences
- Home or auto repair advice
- Family issues
- Planning weddings/showers
- Dreams: career or personal
- Introduction to a new hobby
- Volunteering, Philanthropy
- Starting or running a business
- Financial strategies or lessons

- Dining
- Music
- Legal matters
- Travel
- Gardening
- Children
- Faith lessons
- Recreation
- Sports

Make a mental note of what is missing from that shortlist above. You can probably add other skills from your youth, career, or life experiences.

PONDERING PAUSE:

- What am I talented in (expert) in? _____
- Does my inner circle know I am skilled at that? _____Yes ___ No
- If no, why have I not shared that previously?
  _____
- I have helped someone with my _____skills.
- What hobbies do I enjoy? _____

- Which new hobby or activities would I like to explore?
  _____

- Who have I met that does those activities? _____,
  _____, _____

- Where should I frequent to meet people/ friends that pursue those interests? _____

The Magic of Shared Expertise

Finding someone you want to share your expertise with can be rewarding and life changing. It can propel an acquaintance into a true friendship. Expertise continues to live on after the friendship because those we teach will teach others. Here are six great examples of when someone spotted my need and shared their knowledge and expertise.

- I am eternally grateful to my neighbor, who spotted me crying on my dock and came to help. What I believed to be a huge issue was easily remedied using her brilliant legal recommendations. I gained relief within ten minutes learning there was a solution. She shared her law expertise, and that night we forged a deep trust and a profound friendship.

- A college friend, Randy, stopped his studies to teach me how to look at my car engine and fluids. He taught me essential car maintenance that I still follow today. Sharing his expertise deepened our connection because I then realized he was a kind and patient person.

- Owning my first home in my twenties did not mean I had a clue about how to cook. I remember the day my mother Betsy, brought over groceries and taught me how to prepare an entire thanksgiving meal. Plus, she demonstrated how to host a dinner for ten. I passed her expertise on to my own daughters later.

- My friend Lisa, a serial entrepreneur in her past life, was the key person who planted the seed to start the Red Hawk Strategic Solutions Company. She pushed me to see something I never considered. Her expertise and wisdom, combined with her zeal and desire for me to succeed, created an entirely new chapter in my life. I will always be grateful to Lisa for boldly sharing her expertise.

- A newer friend to me at that time, Lena, shared her tips and tools on how to become a successful author. She generously shared her expertise and during that same luncheon, our friendship rooted. I then realized this book would be published.
- Alice, a strategist and proficient writer, jumped in helping me layout and edit my book proposal. Her focused tips gave me clarity in my message to get this book published.

Sharing Your Expertise is NOT Bragging

Women have been conditioned to separate their professional persona from their social persona. Which means you can know her in one setting and never learn her other hidden talents. That is why women often have entirely different personas based on where you first meet them. They control how much they are willing to share with the audience because of their fear of bragging or not being relatable. Consequently, the world may fail to see their full ability. I've seen colleagues and friends try to introduce new subjects to others and instead of being motivated to ask questions, all they got was blank stares and they shut down. Their brains interpreted the lack of response as meaning "no one is interested in what I enjoy or have tackled." This happens all the time. A positive mindset would say, "This is not the right audience or the people I need to be around. I need friends who uplift and support what I am interested in."

Here is a big question I frequently hear. "How is it that we can be friends with someone for years and never know they are an expert in something I'm also interested in?" When I asked women why they don't openly share their expertise, these are common answers.

- "I could have talked more on that subject but didn't want to say too much."
- "I had more experience than the others talking but didn't want everyone to think I was a showoff. That is why I said so little."
- " I don't want to seem like I am bragging."
- " I have just never told anybody I am great at that thing."

- "I won't mention my skill because I don't have any friends who'd find it interesting."
- "I don't want to monopolize the conversation. If they really knew me as a friend, they'd already know I am skilled in that."
- "If they wanted my help, they would have asked me."

I wonder if they were told it was rude, overstepping, or bragging to talk about themselves. When you know the answer to someone's search or question, it is not intrusive to share. Yet, most people don't share their expertise or background. Could it be a root cause from our school days? Did a teacher say, "Quit raising your hand and give someone else a chance to answer!" When we are in a learning mode and building confidence, if others say, "Don't talk," it can become a habit to stay quiet.

Be Prepared to Share What Makes You Stand Out

So how can you make it clearer to your inner circle and potential friends that you possess unique talents and are willing to share your expertise?

- Write down those qualities, skills, abilities, training, experiences, hobbies, etc., that you possess.
- Now, look at that list and mentally own it! Accept you are qualified to talk to others on those subjects. You don't have to be the best tennis player or volunteer organizer to discuss what you like, and lessons learned. Your background is an entry point to the conversation. Remember, if someone has zero experience on a topic, you know more than they do already!
- If they seem interested, offer to continue the conversation at another time. That shows you are interested in seeing them again and willing to share your knowledge.
- Get a date scheduled to meet the friend again. Remember to initiate the follow-up.
- Be very positive and patient when instructing them to learn something new. They might have been reluctant prior to asking for

any help and could feel intimidated during learning. The more inviting you are, the greater the connection will develop.

- Ask about what other things they like to do or are interested in learning about.
- Identify another mutual interest you'd like to learn about and ask for their help. That allows the friend to reciprocate and shine as the teacher. It balances out your friendship dynamics.

Embracing a bolder approach to sharing your expertise and talents may feel awkward to you at first. However, it will become easier. Once you become more comfortable with casually mentioning what you've been working on or enjoying, conversations flow more organically. You will learn to discuss your fun and interesting experiences from the past. Start with your closest friends and find a topic or interest you believe you've never mentioned before. If there is little interest shown, then casually mention it to another friend later. You could also say this. "I am working on getting better at my _____ and wondered if you knew anyone else who does that too." I used that technique while writing this book. It was my easy method of informing friends and colleagues that I dreamt of writing a book to help others, plus I welcomed meeting their author friends. That technique gently informs your inner circle what consumes your time, opens the door to a conversation, plus gets you some introductions to like-minded potential friends.

Think of *Collecting True Friends* as a movement in your life that you are now connected to. Think of it as a series of actions that need to become habits and when you do so, along the way, you will become that magnet to others. We've all witnessed someone near us (or a celebrity) that possessed magnetism. It is like an invisible force that pulls you toward them, and the closer you get to the person, the more you smile. When you strive to be the best version of you, meaning the one who possesses the qualities and traits others desire in a dear friend, you'll discover an interesting thing happens. Magnetism attaches itself to your person. It makes you shine radiantly to others, just like someone reached over and clicked on a light switch. It will greatly help you in this quest to collect more true friends into your life. Plus, it insulates you from those unsuitable to be closer. As I love to say, "Your goal is to attract those worthy of your time and devotion." You are doing great acquiring friendship skills; let's move onto the next must in *Collecting True Friends,* which is identifying how to become the best version of you.

CHAPTER 13
FINDING YOUR COURAGE TO BE THE
BEST VERSION OF YOU

Your Journey to *Collect True Friends*

Throughout the book, we focused on becoming more observant of those we encounter as potential friends. Then we weaved in, using discernment to judge if someone was worthy of being in your inner circle. To assess if they were a good fit, you learned to compare their traits against your list of desirable qualities. Then we explored ideal ways to fill in the friendship gaps missing amongst your inventory of friends. We talked a good deal about the advantages of inviting a wider variety of types of people into your life. Plus, we explored how roadblocks can create barriers to trying to connect with potential friends. Then we wrapped up how to be the real deal friend by learning how to spot a friend in need, helping them with life challenges, and being bolder, sharing your talents and expertise.

You are nearing the end of the book and the beginning of your journey to build an inner circle of true friends. We have shared considerable information through anecdotal stories, examples, and Pondering Pause activities. By now, you should have a strong feeling what actions work and what to avoid. You have learned how to build an inner circle of genuine friends, worthy of your time and devotion. You learned how to become a true friend in return.

Hopefully, you find yourself ready to employ your friendship-making skills, but we still have one final lesson. The lynchpin that holds everything together is integrity. Integrity is the ability to act consistently with honesty and uphold moral values. It is a crucial value when being the best version of you. Having and demonstrating integrity will attract quality people to you. What does that have to do with *Collecting True Friends*? Everything!

The Virtue that Cultivates Great Friendships

Integrity is a crucial virtue in the art of *Collecting True Friends*. When you have it, good people are drawn to you, while the lack of integrity will repel them. Intending to do the right things in life is not the same as doing them. For the most part, I believe people are good and want to do good. Their actions show their integrity or lack thereof. However, it is crucial to remember others' actions began with their choices. We all face situations where we are forced to decide while knowing our choice will affect the lives of others. Those are the hard times when our integrity is revealed. It happens at the workplace, in our families, or with friendships. It is not easy to always do the right thing. That's why many people make poor decisions and live with regret. Acting with integrity does get easier with practice. It becomes part of you; it is who you are.

Here is an example of a challenging situation thrown at me as a young director. I was filling in for a senior director. There was an employee known for struggling to meet deadlines. Management disliked the man's unsatisfactory work performance and told the previous director to let him go." That never happened. Leadership made it clear this had to happen and held me responsible. I felt my job was at risk but firing the employee did not feel right in my gut. It seemed incredibly unfair. I had a choice. I prayed for strength to overcome my fear of reprisal and to handle the situation with wisdom and integrity. Those were some dark days in my career.

I finally found my courage and decided to do the right thing, no matter what it cost me. I boldly told Human Resources "I will not fire that long-term employee." I announced we would be taking a different course of action. I insisted we unite our efforts, get him some assistance, and help him finish his time in the company and retire. Even though they were shocked at my response, we did just that! The employee's family attended and beamed when we awarded him a fancy watch during his farewell retirement party. I learned so many lessons from that situation. Here are the top four:

- *Never let the meanness of others influence how you treat people.*
  - That lesson was familiar from my experiences when being bullied as the *Little Viking Girl*. Even when personally threatened, you must know you acted as the *best version of yourself*. When you fail to do that, it haunts you forever.
- *You have to do what you think is right, even in the face of bullies.*
  - Leadership did not later reprimand me or fire me for doing what I knew was the right thing.
- Those who aren't brave enough to do horrible things to others may try to get you to do bad things for them. You've all heard the saying of getting someone else to do your dirty work. When that happens, don't be someone else's tool. Especially in friendships. Do not become someone's messenger when they won't confront their own friend.
- When people realize you are a person of integrity, they will stop trying to manipulate you and move on to an easier target. Your good character is powerful. Never forget that truth!

Remember how we talked about potential friends surrounding you everywhere and are observing your actions? I did not realize how many people were curiously watching to see how I would handle that situation. Bravely standing up against senior leadership's directives and acting with integrity drew others closer to me. I gained support from a wider group of colleagues and employees, too. The story of that employee's retirement spread through the company like wildfire. For years after, colleagues mentioned that employee situation and expressed gratitude how he and his family were respected. As a result, several of those observers became my friends outside of work. Once again, potential true friends can be closer than you think. They are watching your actions. When you behave in the *best version of yourself*, you become a magnet, drawing them closer.

It turned out that acting with integrity to the benefit of that employee and his family was equally beneficial to me personally. Much more than I could have imagined.

TRUTH BOMB:

The moral of this true story is integrity is its own reward.

Integrity Combined with Wisdom and Kindness is Powerful!

We've worked on many of the mechanics that make friendships happen. Those techniques work best when combined with your courage and wisdom to be the best version of yourself. As we discussed earlier, wisdom is knowledge combined with experience. Notice how "wisdom" has two parts: knowledge and experience. What happens to us when we only use one part? When we solely use our experience without updated knowledge, we look antiquated. When we solely use our knowledge and have no experience to apply, we look incomplete to others. Yet when we combine our powerhouse of knowledge and what we have experienced in life, we make better decisions. Many times, we have knowledge or experience but forget to combine the two when choosing how to move forward. Integrity combined with wisdom and kindness is powerful. It prevents much regret in life and amplifies your charisma.

Find Your Grit

What's grit? Do you have it? Grit is your battery pack that pushes you forward. It is your drive. It is persistence to prevail. Grit has emotions and feelings and resides deep within your soul. Everyone has experienced reaching deep and finding their grit. Yet we tend to forget it is there as our secret reserve. It sits there ready to tap. Think back to a tight spot in your life when you pulled yourself through those dark days; that is grit.

Those who aren't crystal clear on what they are seeking will continue to keep looking and trying new things while not realizing what they need is clarity. Often, they need grit to find their clarity. You are here because you made a commitment to yourself to gain better friends. Those we call true friends. Those will be the people in your lives that you want to see more and likewise. Why? Because both sides bring enjoyment and something of value into that friendship. That is why it is vital for you to find your courage and actively seek those that best fit your identified qualities in a friend (from Chapter 4). That's the act of *Collecting True Friends*. We discussed (in Chapters 7 and 8) there will be times your integrity will need to dominate all decisions regarding whether you connect or stay connected with someone. If you can find your grit, using your integrity makes that much easier!

Experiences we go through define our grit, like how we build integrity. Grit is woven into our character like muscle memory built from exercising. Your perseverance to want something bad enough will make you go after it. It is in those moments that you reach down and apply your own grit. You might hear some people call that your "why." When your "why" is big enough to *Collect True Friends* you will find you are willing to pay the price with whatever it takes to reach the outcome you desire. Your desire confirms that you do deserve a life filled with amazing, happy, engaging friends that want the best for you. Those are the people who can bring out the best in you and likewise. That is your "why" for *Collecting True Friends*.

By spending the time on you and exploring the methods covered to gain the best friendships, you mentally have already committed to move forward. Committing and staying the course can feel hard at times. Sometimes, you still may feel like you ran into a wall with certain potential friends. You may struggle to distinguish those potential from real friends. That's when you kick in your new skills which we've explored in-depth. Remember to use more of your awareness and discernment skills, do your qualities check, lead with integrity, and muster grit to attack that wall. No obstacle to finding true friends can stand in your way now!

Not all relationship building is easy. If you feel in your heart and soul that you are meant to be friends with that person and they meet your values, stay the course. Don't let something stop you from gaining a friendship you are supposed to cultivate. Find your grit patiently and be open to their friendship. Remember, the timing has to be mutually right for a friendship to launch. Great people are worth your patience.

PONDERING PAUSE:

You want more amazing quality friendships in your life. Right? Then let's evaluate your drive to make that happen.

- How bad do I want it? ___ (From 1: somewhat to 10: very much)
- Am I willing to spend time and energy to focus and commit to identify potential friends? ___ Yes___ Maybe ___ No.
- What does my end game look like? Can I begin to see myself with a true friend within the next year? ___ Yes ___ Maybe ___ No.
- Can I see myself surrounded by more true friends within 5 years? ___ Yes ___ Maybe ___ No.

If you score lots of "Maybe" or "No," do the right things anyway. You may be pleasantly surprised.

Strive to Become an Even Better Version of You
Being the best version of yourself also means noticing and breaking free of things that don't serve you any longer or perhaps have never been in your best interest. For example, I shared such a story previously about my dear friend Dandi. Even though I loved her and enjoyed our time together, staying with that friend was unwise. Why? It was always a train wreck waiting to happen when Dandi was in my life.

Constant drama prevents personal growth. What no longer fits well in your life can be harmful and prevent you from reaching your potential. For example, women are known to wear ill-fitting shoes because they cost a lot or are beautiful. They forget there is another choice. In comparison, you are striving to become the most appealing version of yourself. Remember to notice anything that feels like a poor fit or leaves blisters such as wearing the wrong shoes. Apply your grit and move on. You must walk through one door to see what is on the other side. Great friendships are on the other side for you. Reflect, pray, and, if deemed it no longer makes sense, break free of what limits you from achieving the best version of yourself (Chapter 8 and 10).

PONDERING PAUSE:

- Do I love myself enough to make myself a priority?
- Am I ready to be honest with myself and name the sources causing drama in my life?
- Am I ready to distance myself from the people who interfere or limit me from being the best version of myself?
- Do I see a better version of myself happening this year?
- Can I visualize having a quality inner circle in the next five years?

Make Yourself a Priority and Honor that Decision
Becoming your best, means making yourself enough of a priority to have a few moments, even if only 5--0 quiet minutes each day, to think about if you like where you are in life and who is in your inner circle. Book a time on your busy calendar to meet with yourself. I know that might sound a little weird at first, but we all know that anything that gets done begins with acting purposefully. A plan didn't just magically happen. Someone thought about it and planned a time to put pieces into motion. If I looked at everything you are doing right now in your life, I bet I would find most of your time is spent doing what others expect from you. That leaves little time for your needs. You deserve to make an

appointment on your calendar (or an alert on your phone) to remind you to take the next X minutes just for you. Spend this time focusing on areas you want to make better in yourself, your life, and how you behave as a friend.

Making yourself a priority does require pausing in your busy schedule to concentrate on how you feel. Yes, notice I said how we feel instead of what we think. Women particularly are constantly thinking about everything that needs to be done. It can be exhausting. If we used our primal gut feelings first, before thinking more on something, we'd reach the answer quicker.

I like to imagine our minds surrounded by external conversation bubbles. Each bubble shows a thought. Women walk around with dozens of bubbles filled with our to-do lists. For centuries, humankind has recognized "woman's intuition" as a real thing. It is as a gift. However, I have friends living with a tight chest, upset stomach, or constipation because their inner self keeps sending physical messages of distress, and the brain logically tells them it's something else. That makes any chance for personal growth a challenge. How can we actualize into the "real deal" friend when we are unaware of what's going on in our own bodies?

Happiness is a Choice – It Doesn't Just Magically Happen
If we make time on our calendar to check in with ourselves, it allows us a period of consciousness to evaluate how we feel about our friends, family, occupation, and things in our lives. Likewise, we decide what we want to do to adjust course. Happiness is a choice. Even when situations are dire and we feel stuck, hope prevails when we can believe happiness is possible again. For example, measuring how we feel with a friend, family, God, work, or nature, allows you the temporary clarity to move forward. It pulls you out of the mud that is acting like suction cups to your feet.

That is why happiness is a choice we all must make. I choose happiness in my world! How about you? Putting your "air mask" on first before you take care of others gives you the clarity to decide how happy you want your life to be. When you regain clarity, that's a perfect time to check your gut and heart and listen. They will guide you deeper as you seek your best version of yourself.

Remember when we talked a while back about the danger of practicing "nicety?" If you can be brutally honest in your reflections about how you feel about something or someone, that is when you will discover where to go next in your friendships. We cannot change others' behaviors, only our own. So don't be "nice" when having a heartfelt reflection and conversation with yourself. Be candid and own what you feel, not what you think you should feel.

 PONDERING PAUSE:

Our conduct is defined by the choices we make. Sometimes we show the best versions of ourselves, and other times we wished we had handled the situation differently. Your decisions have outcomes and when people are involved, they can make or break someone's reputation or connection. Take a few moments to reflect and learn what version you have been and what version is possible:

- Can you recall a time with a friend (or family member) when something imploded in your conversation? You said something, they lashed out at you, and you blurted something back.
- Did your words feel like you uncorked the unspoken truth?
- Can you identify what happened that made those words suddenly jump out of your mouth?
- Are you aware of why this situation triggered you to say it rather than waiting?
- Did you feel like you listened enough in the conversation?
- Did you feel like the other person actively listened to you?
- Did you say something you wish you'd never said aloud?

- If you could go back in time, how would you act differently?

Clueless to Change Even When it is Revealed

A while back, a change was being revealed concerning my purpose. My legacy was defining and clarifying itself. I realized I am here to help others build more meaningful relationships in their business and personal lives. I adjusted to align my energies with that related sense of focus.

Being the best version of yourself requires flexibility to handle sudden changes when necessary. We have to listen to our friends, strangers, and God along the way. Why is that necessary? Because others in this big world have messages, they are supposed to share with us to help us in our personal growth. Their messages don't always make sense when we first hear them, but over time, repeated messages will eventually be heard. If we ignore repeated messages, we will limit our ability to become the best version of ourselves. On one occasion I needed clarity, so I said a quick prayer asking, "Can you make your sign super visible so it can get through my clueless head? I am listening now. I promise to listen more but need your guidance and light now. Thank you." Within five minutes a sign appeared, and I realized with certainty, where I needed to listen more. A sceptic might say it was always there, but I missed it until I started looking for it.

Yet when we are set on a course, introducing change can feel challenging. To us extreme planners, it makes us feel clueless because it has interrupted everything in motion. We create a plan, engage in it, and are slow to readjust based on others' keen insight. That happened to me writing this book, for example. Even though I embraced my talents as a trainer and author, I sometimes felt clueless about the next step. There were constant changes in the book's content, flow, and the people involved along the journey. The book's original publishing trajectory changed several times for it to be aligned and published when most needed. Writing this book clarified my mind and purpose, which helped my journey to be a better version of myself. Once I accepted there was a divine design and rhythm to this author's journey that I could not fully understand, everything fell into place by releasing this guidebook.

PONDERING PAUSE:

- Can I recall a time when I wished I had listened better?
- What clues did I miss that later seemed so obvious?
- If that happened today, would I be more receptive to change?
- How will I be more receptive to change or improve who I am?

The Best Version of YOU Starts Today

This book's philosophy is that *Collecting True Friends* happens when we act nobly, lovingly, open-minded, fun, and are appealing. Think of it as a movement that is slowly happening around us. Your actions will begin to change your world and those in your inner circle. Attracting the right individuals in your world is the first step to grow your inner circle in the right direction. But then, ensuring you are worthy of knowing these friends and earning their friendship is what must follow. Remember what we've covered so far. Our goal is to make your next encounter with a potential ideal friend compelling enough that you both want to see each other later. You now have the new skills available to stand out and pull others towards you like a magnet. Remember, *Collecting True Friends* is an action minded habit. It is not a passive approach. It is a mindset where you now know what you want in a friend, are willing to do what it takes to be a true friend and will initiate the relationship into motion.

AN EASY-TO-USE LIFE & TIME MANAGEMENT TOOL:

Here is a Life Management Tool I recommend exploring. It allows you to clarify what you would like to focus on more in your busy life so you can improve. Areas cover seven categories: Fun, Friends, Family, Fitness, Finance, Faith, (career) Field. Daily reminders are provided to move you closer to reaching those goals. Friendship would be a perfect area to "goal yourself up" after reading this book.

https://myoola.oolalife.com/Redhawk is your invitation to explore this fun helpful app, or you may open using the barcode above.

SELECTED REFERENCES, RESOURCES, AND NOTED GREAT READS

Cacioppo, John T., and William Patrick. *Loneliness, Human Nature and the Need for Social Connection.* W.W. Norton & Company, 2009.

Duncan-Hawker, Elizabeth. Author of *Collecting True Friends* has spent decades taking notes from her continual observations while testing what works and does not work, making interactions and building winning relationships. That independent research has been combined with wisdom gained from her hands-on training to over a thousand individuals with her relationship growth system to better connect with others in business sales, events, employees, and meetings. www.growthnetworking.com/.

Gibbons, Serenity. "You and Your Business Have 7 Seconds to Make a First Impression: Here's How to Succeed." *Forbes*, Forbes Magazine, 20 June 2018, www.forbes.com/sites/serenitygibbons/2018/06/19/you-have-7-seconds-to-make-a-first-impression-heres-how-to-succeed/?sh=1e4e8ab356c2.

King, Marissa, and Emma Seppala. "Having Work Friends Can Be Tricky, but It's Worth It ^ h03u05." *HBR Store*, 8 Aug. 2017, store.hbr.org/product/having-work-friends-can-be-tricky-but-it-s-worth-it/H03U05.

Lindenfors, Patrik, et al. "New Study Deconstructs Dunbar's Number (Number of Friends)." *ScienceDaily*, ScienceDaily, 4 May 2021, www.sciencedaily.com/releases/2021/05/210504211054.htm.

"Loneliness Has Same Risk as Smoking for Heart Disease." *Harvard Health*, 16 June 2016, www.health.harvard.edu/staying-healthy/loneliness-has-same-risk-as-smoking-for-heart-disease.

Lowndes, Leil. *How to Talk to Anyone: 92 Little Tricks for Big Success in Relationships*. (Michigan: Brilliance Audio Publications, 2015).

Mcleod, Saul. "Maslow's Hierarchy of Needs." *Simply Psychology*, 29 Dec. 2020, www.simplypsychology.org/maslow.html.

Michail, Jon. "Council Post: Strong Nonverbal Skills Matter Now More than Ever in This 'New Normal.'" *Forbes*, Forbes Magazine, 21 Aug. 2020, www.forbes.com/sites/forbescoachescouncil/2020/08/24/strong-nonverbal-skills-matter-now-more-than-ever-in-this-new-normal/?sh=7ffb7ec75c61.

Schrader, Jessica. "Sympathy vs. Empathy." *Psychology Today*, Sussex Publishers, www.psychologytoday.com/us/blog/click-here-happiness/202007/sympathy-vs-empathy.

Sisco, Lena. *You're Lying! Secrets from an Expert Military Interrogator to Spot the Lies and Get to the Truth*. Career Press, 2015.

Sweeney, Joe, and Mike Yorkey. *Networking Is a Contact Sport: How Staying Connected and Serving Others Will Help You Grow Your Business, Expand Your Influence -- or Even Land Your Next Job*. BenBella Books, 2011.

Tate, Nick. "Loneliness Rivals Obesity, Smoking as Health Risk." *WebMD*, WebMD, 4 May 2018, www.webmd.com/balance/news/20180504/loneliness-rivals-obesity-smoking-as-health-risk.

The State of Loneliness in America - Cigna. www.cigna.com/assets/docs/newsroom/loneliness-survey-2018-updated-fact-sheet.pdf.

ABOUT THE AUTHOR

Elizabeth Duncan-Hawker had to master the art of making and keeping friends at an early age. Today, her magnetism pulls acquaintances closer and puts strangers at ease. She loves to engage all types of people in conversation. *Collecting True Friends* was divinely inspired to help others learn proven methods of creating and developing quality relationships.

A busy entrepreneur, Elizabeth created Growth Networking, a life-changing development program which she uses to train Business Professionals, Entrepreneurs, Boards, and Universities in the techniques of relationship marketing.

The initial goal of the www.GrowthNetworking.com system was to teach business owners how to retain more clients by effectively connecting with them. When participants inquired how to also spot potential friends among the crowd, Elizabeth realized there was a social need to convert a connection from professional to personal. Today, Elizabeth's teachings include ways to cultivate friendships and long-term relationships among those we meet.

She is a co-founder of the successful women's series group, the **Women's Forum of Coastal Virginia**, which has grown to over 500 members in just three years. Elizabeth's networking talents bring people together, and she has been given the title "The Connector." http://womensforumnetwork.com/about.

Elizabeth is actively requested to speak at organizations, forums, and institutions. Earlier in her career, Elizabeth was a strategy and business development executive. She holds a Bachelor's degree from Old Dominion University in Political science and a Master's degree in Business Administration from Strayer University. Additionally,

Elizabeth was recently certified in the Psychology of Leadership from Cornell University.

Elizabeth loves spending time with her diverse collection of true friends. Her husband of 30 years and their large family reside in Virginia Beach Virginia U.S.A. with a collection of big rescue dogs. She sports a sense of adventure, high energy, a desire to travel, and has an engaging style as a connector, strategist, friend, and award-winning speaker.

I believe it is not by mere coincidence that we have met each other. Certain people meet or land together in situations because there is a need to be fulfilled. When that happens, I feel grateful to meet those new people. They may be precisely what you need more of in your life. Remember to use your powers of observation and discernment. It is often in those unplanned moments where we find and *Collect True Friends* worthy of our time and devotion. I am grateful to have spent this time helping you find and *Collect True Friends* in your busy life. I wish you continued blessings in your life.

Please reach out so we can stay connected!

Elizabeth

Let's Connect!!
You may find me at:
https://linktr.ee/theredhawk
https://www.instagram.com/growthnetworking/
www.CollectingTrueFriends.com

We welcome: Speaking Invitations, Book Clubs, Meet the Author Events, and Book Signings.

TO BOOK ELIZABETH
FOR YOUR NEXT EVENT OR BOOK CLUB:

Reach out to MediaCTFriends@gmail.com

Feel free to connect easily with Elizabeth on all social media platforms by opening her bio link at https://linktr.ee/theRedHawk

IF YOU ENJOYED THIS BOOK
Please Post a Review on Amazon at www. Amazon.com

Give a friend a yellow rose and share this book with them to let them know how much you care.

Machines

By Ann Morris   Photographs by Ken Heyman

ScottForesman

A Division of HarperCollins*Publishers*

This machine goes
up, up, up.

This machine goes
round, round, round.

This machine goes
chop, chop, chop.

This machine goes
down, down, down.

6

This machine goes
crunch, crunch, crunch.

These machines go
crash, bam, boom!